Tour de France

_____ Three weeks to glory

Samuel Abt

Frontispiece photo:
On the final circuit of the Tour,
the pack leaves the Arc de Triomphe
behind coming down the
Champs Élysées
(photo Presse-Sports)

Bicycle Books — San Francisco

First printing, 1991

Printed in the United States of America

Published by:
Bicycle Books, Inc.
PO Box 2038
Mill Valley CA 94941

Distributed to the book trade by:
USA: The Talman Company, New York, NY
Canada: Raincoast Book Distribution, Vancouver, BC
UK: Chris Lloyd Sales and Marketing Services, Poole

Cover design:
Kent Lytle
Cover photograph: Jean-Pierre Lenfant (Vandystadt)

Cataloging in Publication Data:
Abt, Samuel
Tour de France, Three weeks to glory
1. Sports — bicycle racing
2. Bicycles and bicycling
3. Authorship
I. Title

Library of Congress Catalog Card Number 91-70410

Hardcover:
ISBN 0-933201-40-0

Paperback:
ISBN 0-933201-39-7

"Bicycle racing was the only sport in the world, he said. Had I ever followed the Tour de France? Only in the papers. The Tour de France was the greatest sporting event in the world. Following and organizing the road races had made him know France. Few people know France. All spring and all summer and all fall he spent on the road with bicycle road-racers. Look at the number of motor cars now that followed the riders from town to town in a road race. It was a rich country and more sportif each year. It would be the most sportif country in the world. It was bicycle road-racing did it."

— Ernest Hemingway

Acknowledgements

For their editorial help and support, I owe thanks to Theodore Costantino and Christopher Koch of *Bicycle Guide* magazine, Joseph Vecchione and Neil Amdur and their caring copy editors at *The New York Times*, and Rob van der Plas, my editor at Bicycle Books.

On the road, I owe thanks to the usual suspects, among them Geoffrey Nicholson, Stephen Bierley, Graham Jones, Salvatore Zanca, Robert Zeller, Phil Liggett, Paul Sherwen, Mike Price, Rupert Guinness and Susan Bickelhaupt. A special debt is owed to the many reporters of *l'Équipe*, who were in all the places no one man could hope to be.

And once more I thank my children, Claire, Phoebe and, this time especially, John. Researching and writing this book without his companionship and assistance would have been much less fun. Exploring Montgeron in a snowstorm without him would have been no fun at all.

This book is dedicated to all the young riders striving to ride in the Tour de France someday.

"Damn Amateurs"

Declan Lonergan was working at the front of the Nissan International Classic in Ireland when Sean Kelly began yelling at him. "Don't do that," Lonergan quoted his fellow Irishman as having said. "Let the bastards do their own work."

A young amateur with the Irish national team, Lonergan had gone off on a breakaway. He was quickly caught by such star riders as Jelle Nijdam, Olaf Ludwig and Kelly. When the three of them continued to attack, Lonergan jumped back into their group and began pulling hard before Kelly yelled at him. The amateur felt flush around the ears, he recalled. "It was embarrassing because they all heard him. But he was right because a few miles further on, just outside Killarney, the hammer came down." At that point, Lonergan was barely able to hang on.

He had limited goals in the Nissan and victory was certainly not among them. As he knows, 21-year-old amateur riders do not beat some of the world's finest professionals and win bicycle races.

So, even after he finished third and then first in the race's first two of 20 road sprints, Lonergan did not allow his hopes to rise.

"I was surprised there," he admitted. "I don't think the pros really took the first day's sprints too seriously. In the one I won, I went into the last corner, still 400 meters to go, and I panicked and just sprinted and they weren't coming around me. So that was grand.

"But the last few days the pros were taking it more seriously and it's a lot harder."

By the time the 84-man field fetched up in Dublin, it had become very hard indeed. Lonergan, a native of Waterford, was far down the overall standings in 78th place, more than 24 minutes behind the winner, Erik Breukink of PDM.

7

On the basis of that first day's efforts, however, he finished 10th in the overall sprints competition. "That's my strength," he said, "sprinting and time trialing. At 75 kilos (165 pounds), I'm too big to be a good climber. Last year in the Nissan my form was slightly better and I finished 35th."

Still he hoped that he had accomplished his primary ambition: to impress the manager of a professional team, any professional team of the 16 among the 19 teams in the race.

"You don't really have to be the best rider in the world to turn professional," Lonergan hoped. "You have to win a few national races and let the managers see what you can do. It's my dream. It's the whole point."

He was not alone in his thinking. Every fall, 40 or 50 amateurs sign their first two-year professional contracts. Comparatively few of them are invited to sign a second contract in a sport that is long in judging a rider's potential by his results. The path is even harder for a neo-professional from outside the traditional bicycle racing strongholds on the Continent. Irishmen, Englishmen, Australians and Americans have usually found themselves consigned to donkey work on their first, and perhaps last, European team.

Lonergan knew the feeling. For the last two seasons he had been riding for the UVC Aube team based in Troyes, France, and won four races in 1990, including the esteemed Bourges race in the Coupe de France-Mavic competition. Yet professional French teams ignored him and signed a teammate instead.

"My team manager says physically he's not as good as I am, but he's French," Lonergan said without obvious bitterness.

The young Irishman had some nationalist advantages of his own: He spent his winters training with Sean Kelly. "I really admire him, have so much respect for him," Lonergan said. "He lives in Carrick-on-Suir, just 17 miles from where I live. He'll say, 'Give us a ring and we'll go for a spin during the week.' We've been doing that the last three years, riding mountain bikes together till Christmas then road bikes till the middle of February, when he goes back to Europe."

Despite their friendship, Kelly had measured praise for Lonergan. "He's one of the best amateur riders in this country," he said. "But he ought to be winning more races. He ought to be doing more."

The manager of Ireland's amateur team, Alisdair Mc-Lennan, agreed. "Lonergan needs this much more," he said, holding his fingers a few inches apart. "He's that close and that far, and the difference is a professional career."

At about Lonergan's age, Kelly left home and moved to Metz, in eastern France, where he rode for an amateur team, won a great many races and attracted the attention of the pros. In his taciturn way, Kelly holds this model up to his compatriot. "He says, 'You've got to do it yourself, I did it myself,'" Lonergan said, "'Give it 100 percent, just like I did.'"

Lonergan accepts that advice, mainly because he has few options if he does not turn professional. "I don't have a trade, I didn't study for anything, so I don't really know what I'll do if I don't make it. And that's why I'm giving it 100 percent."

While he does, he continues to endure the amateur's lot.

"If you say something to most professionals, they just ignore you or give a mumble of an answer. Some just look through you. You feel a bit embarrassed when that happens.

"When the race actually starts, you see those guys suffer and you're suffering as well. It doesn't make you feel good, but it makes you feel more even.

"They were all amateurs once, just like us. I heard this pro, he's an English pro, and the day into Cork one of the amateurs attacked at the start and I heard this pro going, 'Damn amateurs.'

"He was an amateur himself two years ago, and he's probably still wearing the same socks he wore two years ago.

"Damn amateurs," Lonergan snorted.

Table of Contents

Chapter 1
_____ The Awaited Morning

This is the awaited morning. To the east, on a line past the Eiffel Tower, thick clouds begin turning fiery pink in the first sunlight. A cold wind is blowing dead leaves around the streets of Paris. Out in the countryside of France, the fields are brown and barren, their corn long harvested and the stalks chopped down for fodder. Until the stubble is ploughed under when winter wheat is planted, the landscape is bleak and the air full of despair. For professional bicycle racers, April is not the cruelest month. Far from it. In April, hopes for a successful season are as green as the shoots just then starting to push through the fields that the riders pass in their early races. The cruelest month is really October, when the nine-month racing season ends and the riders finally know what they have failed to accomplish.

The one-day classics of spring — the Tour of Flanders, Paris–Roubaix, Milan–San Remo and Liege–Bastogne–Liège, among others — roll past trees in bud, and now those same trees give a name to the final fall classics in France and Italy: 'The Race of the Fallen Leaves,' they call Paris–Tours and the Tour of Lombardy. The leaves have fallen from long lines of plane trees in every small town along the route.

Another week or two will finish the racing season. But here, today, on this awaited morning in October, the next racing season will be born. The roads of all the world's bicycle races lead toward one site only: the Tour de France. "The Tour stands alone," says Erik Breukink, a Dutch rider. "There, everybody is watching you. The whole world watches." And today the organizers of the world's biggest, richest, most-important and best bicycle race will unveil the route of the next Tour de France.

For months everybody has known that Lyon will be the start of the 1991 Tour and that Paris will be the finish; the lines between them, even the direction, clockwise or counter, have remained secret. They will become known at the presentation of the 78th Tour de France.

All is ready in the southwestern Paris suburb of Issy les Moulineaux, where the daily sports newspaper *l'Équipe* had moved to a few years ago. The presentation will be staged in Issy's Palais des Arts et des Congress and a banner has been stretched across the street leading to the 'palace,' a meeting hall in dreary and heavily official style. 'Arrivée,' Finish, says the banner, dangling the red triangle that marks the final kilometer in each stage of the Tour. The Tour's organizers have done their best to replicate their summer kingdom: the same signs that mark each final dash to the line — 100, 50, 25 meters — stand sentry on this street, the Avenue Victor Cresson. The same green arrows of July point to the press room, the same yellow arrows designate parking for officials.

Tour officials in identical forest-green blazers and dark grey trousers jostle for attention and welcome their guests. The red cars used by these officials are parked, as always, with no respect for ordinary law; the Tour sets its own laws, and so the cars block the sidewalk. A few shoppers grumble and an old woman even shakes a fist at the latest driver to jump the curb. He smiles back, knowing full well that the bicycle race comes first, far ahead of such mundane concerns as being able to pass on the sidewalks. Where the Tour is, there is no Issy les Moulineaux. In the kingdom of the Tour, there is only the Tour.

In the hall where the Tour will soon be presented, a slide show displays international press coverage, rotating Page Ones from French, Belgian, Dutch, Canadian, Japanese, Spanish, Italian, Portuguese, Irish, British, American and German newspapers and magazines. Interspersed are scenes from the Tour — the riders struggling up mountains, along roads painted with their names, down the straightaway in a final sprint, past a field of sunflowers. "The three biggest media sports events in the world are the Olympic Games, the World Cup of soccer and the Tour de France," announces Jean-Pierre Carenso, the director of the race's commercial operations. "Next year the Olympics and the World Cup take a well-deserved rest, leaving the field entirely free to the Tour de France. There will be only us." The remark is greeted with affectionate laughter, as if the 1,200 people in this hall could imagine admitting that the Tour de France suffers competition.

Carenso then helps present a trophy to Greg LeMond for winning the previous Tour. "I hope I'm back to get it again next year," LeMond jokes. He is applauded by the guests, mainly journalists, Tour officials and politicians from the many towns, cities and regions through which the race will pass. The guests revel in the ambiance of the Tour. This is their world: the sport of summer. They seem uncomfortable in their suits and ties, so different from the shorts and T-shirts they wear three weeks a year, in Tour time.

Roger Legeay, the *directeur sportif* of the Z team, passes down the aisle, smiling, delighted to be the coach of the rider who won the last Tour. In this world, coaches are stars too: Bernard Vallet of RMO, Maurice le Guilloux of Toshiba, Jan Gisbers of PDM strut through the crowd. LeMond is joined by a few other riders: Laurent Fignon, Stephen Roche, Marc Madiot, Claudio Chiappucci, Gianni Bugno and Gilles Delion. If asked, they would probably agree with the judgment of Henri Manders, a Dutch journeyman with the Helvetia team based in Switzerland. "I don't race for the *ambiance*," he is quoted as saying in *l'Équipe* this very morning. He rides for the glory, the prize money and the victories. The rest of those in the hall, the journalists especially, have few chances for glory, prize money and especially victories, and so they settle happily for ambiance.

Being together with colleagues, exchanging gossip, catching each other up on what's been happening since the last race — ambiance. Working with friends, sharing a quote from a rider, making plans for dinner once a story has been sent — ambiance. (The choice of Lyon for the start pleases everybody because it is so easy there to eat well. Eating well is part of the ambiance, an important part; two reporters for the newspaper *Le Telegramme* of Brest argued heatedly in their car a few Tours ago when each discovered that the other had failed to pack a *Guide Michelin* listing the best restaurants throughout France. "Imbecile," shouted one reporter, "because of you we starve." When a guest in their car pointed out that they could buy the Michelin that night at the end of the Tour's first stage, the other immediately objected: "But how will we know where to have lunch?")

The slide show ends and Jean-Marie Leblanc, director of operations for the race, takes the stage. After a few words of welcome he presents the map of the 78th Tour de France.

First the highlights: The race will start July 6 in Lyon and end in Paris on July 28. During those three weeks it will cover about 3,940 kilometers in a counterclockwise direction, leaving France for a day, July 18, on a visit to Jaca, Spain. One day off is scheduled, July 17, but it will include a plane flight from St. Herblain in Brittany to Pau, the gateway to the Pyrenees. Bicycle-mad regions of France, like the North and Brittany, will get their fill of the race, while such traditional stops as Bordeaux and the Massif Central will be skipped. Three days have been added to the usual first week over level territory, delaying until July 18 the first climbing. Continuing their efforts 'to modernize,' as the Tour's organizers phrase it, they have also reduced the number of individual time trials. Excluding the short prologue, the riders face two individual races against the clock instead of the usual three. Neither of the time trials will be uphill, another break with tradition.

The Flat Earth Society seems to have subverted the Tour. Just four days will be spent in the high mountains and, of the two days in the Pyrenees and two days in the Alps, just one of each appears to be truly daunting. Even the fearsome climb to Alpe d'Huez has been leveled by removing the usual towering peaks earlier in the stage. Instead of a 25-kilometer climb up the 1,993-meter-high Madeleine, followed by an 18-kilometer climb up the 1,951-meter Glandon, as in 1990, or the 2,556-meter Galibier, followed by the 2,080-meter Croix de Fer, as in 1989, Alpe d'Huez will be preceded in 1991 by the Bayard, a climb of 7.5 kilometers to an altitude of 1,248 meters, and the Ornon, a climb of 5 kilometers to an altitude of 1,360 meters.

In sum, 11 stages will be on the flat, four will be hilly, four will be in the high mountains, and four will be time trials, including the prologue and the team time trial. Leblanc explains that a balance has been sought between long stages (more than 230 kilometers) and short ones (less than 170 kilometers) and that there will be six of each.

The point is clearly to seek parity. Many more riders will make it through the mountains in position to battle it out for the final victory. As LeMond has pointed out, nearly all riders can handle one day in the high mountains and many can handle two, but the third day is the killer. Now the two days have been cut back to fractionally more than one. Still, conventional wisdom says that the riders, not the course, make the race. Three of the last four Tours have been decided no earlier than the next-to-last day, so the organizers must be doing something right.

Leblanc now goes into details, taking the audience through each stage audiovisually. There will be stops in big cities, of course, including Dijon, Le Havre, Rennes, Pau and Gap, as well as such small places as Bron, Argentan, Ales, Castres, Lugny and Melun. With the giant screen illuminated behind him, he announces that 22 teams of 9 riders each will again be invited. Sixteen teams will be selected according to their standings in the computerized ranks of the International Federation of Professional Cycling as of May 21, 1991 and six wildcards will be distributed on June 18. Ten million French francs (then $2 million) will be given in prizes, with two million francs to the winner, who traditionally shares it with his teammates.

Leblanc calls for questions. Will bonus seconds be attributed to winners? Only until the Tour reaches the mountains. Why will there be no uphill time trial? Not to penalize those riders who do not climb well. Will the race pass over any of the cobblestones that make Paris–Roubaix such a terror? No, the cobblestoned roads are too narrow to permit such a risk at this level of competition. Why has Le Havre

15

been included as a stage finish instead of some other city in Normandy? Why not? There were three times more candidate cities for arrivals or departures than there were such points, Leblanc says. Why have Marseilles and the whole of Provence and the Côte d'Azur been excluded? Unfortunately the Tour de France is allotted only three weeks on the international calendar and time and distance do not permit visits everywhere. Perhaps next year or the one after that.

Then Hervé Mathurin of the newspaper *Sud Ouest* challenges the organizers by asking if they have forever ruled cobblestones out of the race. Like so many questions about the Tour, this is spoken in a code understood only by insiders. Mathurin is really asking whether the race has permanently changed its face by dropping a principal difficulty. Cobblestones have rarely been included since the early 1980s, when the lightweight Colombians became the first 'outside' nation admitted to the Tour in its drive to internationalize the sport. In 1983, their first year in, the Colombians lost great amounts of time as they gingerly picked their way through the huge, irregular and unfamiliar cobbles. The next year, with the Colombians still in, the cobbles were out. Now the Colombians have become a minor team, with their stars riding for Spanish teams, and the cobblestones are still missing. Mathurin is asking metaphorically if one of the old-fashioned challenges of the Tour de France is no longer considered relevant.

The answer, as might be expected, does not address that point. "Absolutely no, the cobblestones have not been banned forever," says a Tour official. "But they will be included only when the road is wide enough for the Tour de France." In other words, the few ancient cobblestoned roads of the North not yet tarred over cannot be used, but if a new, three-lane, cobblestoned road is built, the Tour de France will make sure it is fit in.

The answer is a death knell for traditionalists. For them, an undemanding Tour de France is a contradiction in a sport that has elevated — made understandable — suffering and sacrifice. Life is not so hard, the Tour's organizers are saying, and this is no longer the age of heroes. We worship comfort, even luxury, rather than effort. We strive for the easy road and the easier dollar. We present just enough difficulties but no longer ask the riders to exceed themselves so often. We are modern and the Tour de France has been modernized.

There is much grumbling among those who have understood the question and the answer.

Looking at the map with other eyes, those of a man who will have to ride the full 3,940 kilometers, LeMond says that he likes the course. "It looks good to me, it looks ideal," he announces. Then he admits, "I say that every year."

L'Envoi

Outside, after the presentation, the cold wind of autumn continues to whip the dead leaves around the street. But for those filing out of the building, it is summer again.

The sky is a washed blue and the heat has just started to burn the dew off the fields of sunflowers along the route. In the main square of whichever small town or big city the Tour de France is starting from this morning, the riders are filing up to the daily sign-in. The crowd feels a rush of excitement as the race's announcer, Daniel Mengeas, finds something worthy to say for each rider, however undistinguished his career may have been. A low-ranking domestique from Spain? "The revelation of the Tour of Valencia this spring." A sprinter who has lost his ambition and power? "The always dangerous Belgian, a man his rivals know they must watch as the finish line approaches." A climber who has come in far behind on the first day in the Alps? "A man who never has two bad days in a row in the mountains, and that spells trouble for the others."

After all, these are the riders of the Tour de France, heroes all in a heroic tradition.

"I believe that the Tour is the best example we have ever encountered of a total, hence an ambiguous, myth.... The epic expresses that fragile moment of history in which man, however clumsy and deceived, nonetheless contemplates through his impure fables a perfect balance between himself, the community and the universe." — Roland Barthes.

Chapter 2
_____ An Enduring Gamble

The Auberge Reveil Matin, or the Alarm Clock Inn, is there still, just where the road from Paris enters Montgeron. The *auberge* is made of stucco now, with false wooden beams embedded in its long walls in the Norman style. There is no sign that the *auberge* rents rooms, but its dining room offers a 140-franc menu of three courses. (It's probably better to stay away from such chic choices as *tournedos Rossini* and sweetbreads Grandma's way and order instead the steak with fried potatoes, like most of the Sunday lunch crowd.)

As towns go, Montgeron is standard among the southeastern suburbs of the capital: some charming villas in the shadows of apartment houses, the usual butchers, bakers and pizzerias, the Victor Duruy primary school with a sapling — 'the Tree of Liberty' — planted out front to celebrate the 1989 bicentennial of the French Revolution. Are the schoolchildren taught that Thomas Jefferson said the tree of liberty had to be watered with the blood of tyrants?

A main square holds St. Jacques church, the town hall and the police station. Behind a huge monument to the town's dead of both world wars lies a graveyard. Another graveyard waits down the main road, the Avenue de la République, which soon changes its name to the Avenue Jean Jaurès. Nothing much appears to happen here. People say that nothing has ever happened in Montgeron.

They are wrong there. The Auberge Reveil Matin is where,

at 3 o'clock in the afternoon of July 1, 1903, the first Tour de France began.

A plaque in the *auberge's* wall facing the expressway into Paris testifies to that beginning, but fails to explain why Montgeron was chosen. The bartender in the Auberge Matin Reveil is no help. "I couldn't say," he answers. "I wasn't around then." Nobody is left who was around then. At the offices of *l'Équipe*, the staff historian can say only that the prefect of police in Paris refused to permit the first Tour to start or end in Paris proper. Thus Montgeron at one end and Ville d'Avray, another suburb, at the other. But why specifically Montgeron? It is one of the many questions about the history of the Tour that are lost in the abyss of French journalism, always so long on color and so short on fact. Even when they do offer dates, times and names, histories of the Tour tend to contradict each other.

All accounts agree on this: The Tour de France began as a gimmick to boost circulation for the newspaper *l'Auto*. Some accounts add that the Dreyfus case, that Belle Epoque scandal involving charges of treason and anti-Semitism, was really at the root of the Tour. Using the two newspapers he edited, the *Petit Journal* and *le Vélo*, Pierre Giffard was one of the few journalists to side with Émile Zola and defend Captain Alfred Dreyfus against the attacks of the Establishment. His impassioned articles in *le Vélo* especially rankled Adolphe Clément, a major manufacturer of bicycles, and the Count de Dion, a *Vélo* financial supporter, who helped set up a rival to the paper in October 1900. They chose for their editor Henri Desgrange, a former bicycle racer who set the first unpaced record for the hour in 1893 and later became a publicity agent for Clément's bicycle factory. The new paper, *l'Auto-Vélo* faced a difficult time in a field crowded with a dozen sports papers and magazines; *le Vélo*, printed on green pages, had a daily circulation of 80,000 copies, a formidable position built on Giffard's flair in originating the Paris–Brest–Paris race in 1891 and revitalizing Bordeaux–Paris in 1902.

Under Desgrange, *l'Auto-Vélo* jumped right into the fight. Only six pages and printed on yellow paper, it attracted a fair share of advertising but could not get its circulation above 20,000 daily. No trick seemed to work, even when Desgrange staged his own Bordeaux–Paris race in 1902, running it a day after Giffard's and using the same route — if not the same riders on the nearly 600-kilometer course.

Giffard and *le Vélo* appeared to be unassailable, especially after they won a lawsuit for plagiarism that obliged *l'Auto-Vélo* to drop the *Vélo*, or bicycle, from its name on January 15, 1903. That was bound to hurt in the circulation battle, since bicycle racing was a major and mass sport, while automobile races were mainly curiosities for the elite who could afford cars and an interest in them.

Four days later, Desgrange struck back.

By today's newspapering standards, his one-column headline at the top of Page One was minimal display. 'Le Tour de France,' it said. Underneath, in small type, was the headline's bank in a reverse pyramid: "The greatest bicycling test in the world — A monthlong race — Paris–Lyon–Marseille–Toulouse–Bordeaux–Nantes–Paris — 20,000 francs in prizes — Leaving June 1. Arriving in Paris July 5 at the Parc des Princes."

The article below, signed by Desgrange, noted that if the name of his newspaper had been changed, the announcement of the race proved that its coverage, "which consists of not neglecting any sport," had not. Most of the article was given over to listing the prizes for each stage. The impressive total of 20,000 francs (then $100,000) would be roughly equal in buying power now to 3.2 million francs. The entire distance would be 2,200 kilometers, covering three-fourths of France, and riders could sign up either for the full race or for one or more stages. Further details would be made public soon to the readers of *l'Auto*, Desgrange promised.

The announcement caused "an enormous emotion in the sports world," *l'Auto* reported the next day in a Page One article signed by the paper's chief cycling correspondent, Géo Lefèvre. "Naturally, champions of the road now in Paris paraded into our offices, enthusiastic about the idea and thrilled by such a manna of prizes," Lefèvre continued.

His article the day after reported equally enthusiastic reaction by other newspapers, *le Vélo* excluded. *Le Figaro* was certain "this great race will cause a sensation by its enormous length." *Le Matin* felt "the race is sure to be a success and bring honor to its organizers." As *l'Auto* noted, the other papers "all agreed in finding this Tour de France 'enormous,' 'grandiose,' 'a monster,' 'gigantic,' 'sure to make a sensation'."

To read *l'Auto* nearly 90 years later, even discounting the self-promotion, it is easy to see that the idea of the race truly was a sensation. Sportsmen in cities to be visited sent letters celebrating the news. On the other hand, Desgrange reported on January 25, many cities complained that the Tour would miss them. "Perpignan, in a tearful letter, insists that it isn't far from the projected route," he wrote. Albi, Cahors and Auch, "with a touching unanimity," protested that they had not been included. So did Cognac, Niort and Limoges.

Desgrange had found the right formula — a race nearly twice as long as the record holder, Paris–Brest–Paris, and far richer and more prestigious than any other. As Lefèvre put it, "the triumph of the winner will be that he did not win simply Paris–Lyon or Marseille–Toulouse or Bordeaux–Nantes, but the race of the Tour de France."

For all his drive and single-mindedness — "he was a tough man and a tough man to work for," Lefèvre remembered decades later about the employer usually known as H.D. — Desgrange had of course not come up with the idea of the Tour in the four days after his newspaper's name was amputated. Although he came to be known as "the father of the Tour," Desgrange hadn't come up with the idea at all, according to most historians.

One of them, Pierre Chany, the veteran *l'Équipe* cycling writer, says in his book *Le Tour de France* that in November 1902 Desgrange summoned Lefèvre and other *l'Auto* reporters and editors to his office and complained that something had to be done about Giffard and *le Vélo*.

"The first to answer was Lefèvre," Chany wrote. "What if we organize a race that lasts several days — longer than all of those that exist now? Something like the six-day races on the track, but on the road."

"Until then silent, a man whose name history, alas, has forgotten, opened his mouth, incapable of containing himself and his irony: 'If I understand you, sir, you propose nothing less than a tour of France.'

" 'Why not?' Lefèvre answered."

Desgrange mulled this over and then invited Lefèvre to join him for lunch at the nearby Brasserie Zimmer on the Boulevard Montmartre. Toward the end of the meal, Desgrange returned to the idea of a vast race, saying, "Thousands of kilometers by bicycle, no matter what the weather, on our terrible roads! You'll kill the riders."

"Not necessarily," the reporter answered.

"How many stages do you think it will take? Have you thought about the security? And how much will it cost the organizers?"

"I haven't come up with anything better," Lefèvre admitted. "And, if we succeed, Giffard will be sick with envy."

Promising to think it over, Desgrange later discussed the plan with the paper's financial officer, Victor Goddet. "Goddet studied the project, its prizes and possibility of success, its publicity value, and opened his money box with pretty good grace, it seems," Chany concluded.

Other accounts differ in details. Some histories neglect to mention the sardonic fellow, known only to God, who first called the race the Tour de France. In an account written in 1953, Lefèvre himself even fails to mention the meeting and the lunch. He says of Desgrange, "Was it him, was it me who, one day, said to the other, 'What if we made a Tour de France?' 'Too long. We'll kill the riders, no one will finish.' 'We'll cut the race into stages.' 'But that will cost a lot.' "

By 1953 — and certainly by 1991 — it was too late to remake history. Like the Auberge Reveil Matin, the Brasserie Zimmer, now the Brasserie Madrid, has a plaque. It proclaims that the Tour was born in that room on November 20, 1902.

Whatever the truth, the Tour had a difficult birth. Even Desgrange was forced to admit this early in May, when he wrote that he had thought of calling the whole thing off because barely more than a dozen riders had signed up. Without at least 50 riders, there would be no Tour de France, he warned. Realizing that a major obstacle was that few men wanted to be away from home for 35 days, Desgrange decided to reduce the race's length to three weeks, the same time span still used today.

The definitive plan listed six stages covering 2,428 kilometers with up to four rest days between stages. Racers could compete in the overall Tour or any number of stages, riding far into the night to finish. This new plan attracted to Montgeron 60 riders, of whom 21 finished on July 19, led by Maurice Garin in 94 hours 33 minutes, an average speed of 25.6 kilometers an hour. Second, 2 hours 49 minutes behind, was Louis Pothier.

The 32-year-old Garin, winner previously of Paris–Roubaix, Bordeaux–Paris and Paris–Brest–Paris, was exactly the prominent and colorful rider Desgrange needed to build interest in the Tour: a native-born Italian who had come to France as a boy and was traded by his father to a chimney sweep for a wheel of cheese. "The Little Chimney Sweep," Desgrange dubbed him, the first in a line of Giants of the Road, as riders are still sometimes called in *l'Équipe*, the name *l'Auto* uses now.

With the first Tour a success, the paper's circulation began to rise. (*l'Équipe's* usual 300,000 circulation increases by at least a third during today's Tours.) For the 1904 race, Desgrange did little fiddling other than dropping the rule that a rider could compete in individual stages and adding one that eliminated riders arriving far behind the main field.

A year later, 88 riders left in the second Tour, which was conducted over the same course for 21,000 francs in prizes. The race was a disaster. The first time out, cheating was limited to some outdistanced riders' hauling themselves and their bicycles onto trains to finish a stage. In 1904, cheating was rampant, with crowds of toughs blocking the roads at night, beating some riders, while allowing their favorites through. Nails were strewn on the road, puncturing even the tires on Desgrange's car as he attempted to return the race to control. Charges were heard that some riders had traveled by car at night on difficult stretches of the road.

Garin was again the winner, followed by Pothier, César Garin, Maurice Garin's brother, and Hippolyte Aucouturier, the winner of four of the six stages. Four months later, after an investigation by French cycling authorities, they were all disqualified and first prize was awarded to Henri Cornet, at 20 still the youngest winner of the Tour. Pothier was suspended for life and Maurice Garin for two years. What their offenses were has never been made public.

Publicly distraught, Desgrange was absolute in his declaration that this was the end of the Tour. "The Tour de France is finished," he wrote, "and the second edition, I'm afraid, will be the last. It has been killed by success, by the blind passions it has unleashed, the injuries and filthy suspicions caused by the ignorant and the wicked."

The Tour ended? In his heart, Desgrange didn't believe it for a minute.

And he was right. Occasionally a stage would be interrupted and even halted by political demonstrations and rider strikes, but the Tour itself has never been stopped except by both world wars — there was no race from 1915 through 1918 and again from 1940 through 1946.

Going with the Times

Desgrange, in fact, announced quickly enough that he would continue "the great moral crusade of bicycle racing." As part of that effort, he made many changes in the 1905 Tour. The route was enlarged, adding excursions into Brittany, Normandy and Alsace, and the length grew to 2,975 kilometers divided into 11 stages. The stages themselves were shortened and night stages were eliminated. Overall time no longer decided the winner; in a system that was used until 1913, the winner would be chosen on the basis of points determined by the riders' times.

Finally, Desgrange thought his race was ready to meet the

mountains.

The first was the Ballon d'Alsace and then came two climbs in the Alps, the Laffrey hill and the Bayard pass. The public wondered if racers could ride up the mountains or whether they would have to dismount and walk their bicycles up. René Pottier answered the question by mounting the Ballon d'Alsace at a speed of 20 kilometers an hour and adding to the legend of the Giants of the Road. That he had to quit the next day because of tendinitis did not diminish the legend much.

Bit by bit, Desgrange was fashioning the Tour in its modern image. In 1907 the race was opened to other bicycle manufacturers besides Peugeot, which had enjoyed a near-monopoly after Garin's victory on a La Française model. At first manufacturers were allowed to sponsor individual riders and drive their team cars closely behind; by 1912 the manufacturers were allowed to sponsor teams.

Competition grew intense as each trade team labored to produce the winner of the Tour for advertising reasons. Mistrusting the influence that the trade teams were having on the race, Desgrange could only sympathize that year when Octave Lapize of the Française team suddenly quit in the Pyrenees to protest what he said was a cabal of Belgian riders on different teams conspiring to help Odile Defraye and his sponsor, the potent Alcyon bicycle maker.

But 18 years were to pass before Desgrange found a way to deal with sponsors. Although nothing could be proved, trade teams appeared to be strangling the race throughout the 1920s with their 'arrangements' of winners after long breakaways from unresponsive packs. Desgrange tried different approaches, including introducing time bonuses at the finish (1923) and sending teams off at different times in stages on the flat (1927), turning the Tour for days into a sort of continuous team time trial.

Late in 1929, he decided to revolutionize the race, ending competition by sponsored teams and introducing national and regional teams. For the 1930 race, the 100 riders were divided into 5 teams of 8 men each from France, Italy, Spain, Belgium and Germany plus 60 riders representing the North,

Southeast, Ile de France, Champagne, the Midi, the Côte d'Azur, Normandy, Provence and Alsace-Lorraine. Compensating for the loss of sponsors' fees, Desgrange added a publicity caravan of trucks and cars advertising everything from candy bars to cheese.

The publicity caravan persists to this day as a garish and necessary harbinger of the Tour. Garish? Where else but the Tour do cars carry statues of dead mosquitoes (Catch bug spray) on their roofs? Or whiz through towns to the diesel toot of railroad trains (the French national train system)? Necessary? Crowds line up hours in advance of the riders to snatch at the leaflets and free samples hurled from the speeding publicity caravan. Each piece of paper is studied — the handbills about old-age annuities and furniture sales, the brochures about money to be made in savings accounts or the advantages of joining the army. The free samples set off a scramble for small packets of a breakfast drink, chocolate bars and balloons. Teenage girls wave at each car beseechingly, like some Cinderella hoping to flag down her prince, but the publicity caravan speeds on, littering the roads of France and offering a diversion until the riders arrive and pass in a whirl of wheels. Besides, it helps pay the Tour's bills.

The system of national and regional teams helped reinvigorate the Tour during the 1930s and was continued after World War II until 1962, when trade teams were revived. In 1967 and 1968, the race again turned to national teams, but in 1969 the experiment was abandoned and trade teams have competed ever since. Now they are rarely sponsored by bicycle manufacturers, carrying instead the banners of electronic companies, carpet salesmen, do-it-yourself hardware franchises, clothing factories and storm-window suppliers. The arguments for trade teams include the dilemma of divided loyalties — a Belgian rider, say, who happens to ride most of the year for a Dutch team would find himself competing against his usual teammates in the most important race of them all. How should he respond in a breakaway by his habitual team leader, now on another side? That is a question that sometimes confuses the one-day world championship road race, the only professional competition involving national teams.

In 1936, an ailing Desgrange, who was to die four years later, yielded his direction of the Tour to Jacques Goddet, the son of Victor Goddet, *l'Auto's* original financial director. Goddet continued in that role for 51 years, sharing the responsibilities after World War II with Félix Lévitan, and allowing the race to benefit from continuity at the top for an astounding 84 years.

Only in a few ways would today's Tour de France be unrecognizable to Desgrange. The man who created the leader's yellow jersey in 1919 and the king of the mountains classification in 1933 would not be surprised to see also the green points jersey (1953). From the first individual time trial (1934) it is not too far to the first prologue (1967) nor is it from the start in Montgeron to the first start outside France (Amsterdam, 1954). He would surely understand the change in the finish from a velodrome in Paris, either the Parc des Princes of his day or La Cipale (1968) to the Champs-Elysées (1975) and its traditional half-million spectators.

Might Desgrange be amazed at the way the sport has become truly international? Not really, since he witnessed victories by the first riders from Luxembourg (François Faber, 1909), Belgium (Odile Defraye, 1912) and Italy (Ottavio Bottecchia, 1924). So Desgrange probably would have hailed the first team from outside Europe (Colombia, 1983), the first from America (7-Eleven, 1986) and the first from the Soviet Union (Alfa Lum, 1990). Less certain would be his reaction to the start of the Tour de France every two or three years outside the mother country (the '92 Tour will start in Spain).

The vastness of the race would be familiar. Limited now by international rules to 200 riders, usually divided into 22 teams of 9 men each, the pack is no more than a quarter larger than any that Desgrange watched. In size, prestige and richness of prizes, the Tour remains paramount.

The Giro d'Italia is a fine race to win, but the man who did so in 1990, Gianni Bugno, admitted "The Tour de France is the summit. The fans, the attention, the pressure — everything is bigger." The world championship is another splendid victory, but as Allan Peiper, an Australian, said of the Tour de France: "This is the real world championship. The other just shows who's best for one day."

"In the Tour, everybody is watching you, everybody cares about how you're doing," says the Dutch rider Erik Breukink. "The pressure is enormous but the victory is enormous too."

"There's no race like the Tour," Greg LeMond says. "Everything is bigger, more important."

'Enormous,' 'bigger,' 'more important,' 'the summit' — echos of the words *l'Auto* used in 1903 to announce its first Tour.

In Memoriam: The Women's Tour de France

One part of the race that would surely have puzzled Henri Desgrange was the shortlived *Tour de France Féminin*, the Women's Tour de France (1984–89). As a nobel experiment, it ranked with Prohibition and was nearly as popular.

The Women's Tour de France course was modeled on the men's, covering part of the same daily stages, roughly the last third, a few hours before the men came through. International bicycle racing rules limited women to racing 80 kilometers a day when the Women's Tour started; they were also excused from climbing the highest mountains and their prizes were worth only a 25th of what the men could earn.

While it lasted, the Women's Tour de France never did amount to much of a race. Since few journalists could afford the time to watch them, having instead to be with the real Tour, the women raced virtually without publicity. Another problem, and really the major one, was that the women fell into three rankings: Jeannie Longo alone at the top, Maria Canins a good notch below her, and everybody else far distant.

After a victory in the initial Women's Tour by Marianne Martin of the United States, Longo and Canins — both of

28

whom had missed the inaugural — won all the rest or finished second to each other. Canins, an Italian, triumphed in 1985 and '86, and Longo thereafter until the race was severed from the Tour de France and added to the Tour of the European Community in the fall. Before she retired from the sport late in 1989, Longo had a way of smothering the competition and even the interest in women's racing.

"I learned from the Americans at the Olympic Games in '84," she said at the 1989 world championships as she summed up her philosophy. "They always said, 'Go for it, go for the win.'"

Go for the win is what Longo did for years with stunning and stultifying success. When she cruised across the finish line an easy victor in the '89 world championship, she had recorded her fourth victory in five years. It was also her third gold medal that year, after the one in the individual pursuit for the third time out of four tries, and a gold in the points race.

Longo dominated French racing for a decade, and international racing for half that time. For many of those years she feuded with French riders and cycling officials, dictating who her coaches and teammates would be. The only coach she trusted, she often said, was her husband, Patrice Ciprelli, although his credentials were regarded as dubious by the bicycle racing community.

With many a mutter, the French always accepted her demands since she was a winner. Along with her road-race and pursuit medals in the world championships and her triumphs in the last three Women's Tour de France, she won the Coors Classic in 1985, '86 and '87. She held the women's hour records indoors, at altitude and at sea level; the records for 5, 10 and 20 kilometers outdoors; and for 3, 5 and 20 kilometers indoors. Her only failure had been at the Olympic Games, where she never won a medal.

Longo's obvious successor when she quit at 31 was not Canins, then in her 40s, but another Frenchwoman, Catherine Marsal, then 18. Second to Longo in that world championship, and the easy winner of the race in 1990, she also won the junior world championship on the road in 1987 and in the pursuit in 1988.

Although they were teammates, Longo and Marsal were not friends. Longo was not close to any member of her final world championship team, which imposed a fine of 10 francs on anybody who mentioned her name at the communal dining table. Longo ate and trained apart from the team, of course.

Another reason for her teammates' anger was Longo's refusal to ride in the team time trial, in which the French finished third. "I'm not a superwoman," Longo said in her own defense, but really she was.

Chapter 3
_____ Legends of the Giants

Nurtured by Henri Desgrange, the legends of the Giants of the Road sprung from the first Tour. What he wanted were heroes and he set the bar ever higher to create them.

In 1910, when he added the Pyrenees to the Tour's route, the riders denounced 'the circle of death' of the Peyresourde, Aspin, Tourmalet and Aubisque Passes. These mountains, they charged, were so wild that they were still roamed by bears. Desgrange was unyielding and approved a climb over the 1,700-meter-high Aubisque even after an agent said that the road up to the pass was no more than a mule track.

On the day of the stage, the editor waited with other officials at the bottom of the mountain for hours past the expected arrival of the riders. Finally one appeared but would not or could not speak. Fifteen minutes later came Octave Lapize, the Frenchman who was to win that Tour. Lapize stared at Desgrange and spat out the word 'Assassin.' By all accounts, Desgrange was pleased.

Another great legend dates from 1913, when the vastly popular Eugène Christophe, then in second place overall, broke the front fork of his bicycle on a descent from the Tourmalet. As the rules specified, he had to repair the damage himself, so he picked up his bicycle and walked 14 kilometers to the nearest village, Ste. Marie de Campan, where he found a blacksmith's shop and proceeded to forge the needed piece. The work went on for four hours while the officials who were overseeing his labor began to fidget with hunger. "Have _I_ eaten?" cried Christophe.

Finished at last, he rode on to rejoin the Tour, all hope of winning gone. Only later did he learn that he had been penalized an extra three minutes for allowing a small boy to work the bellows while he had both hands full hammering the new fork.

Lightning struck twice for Christophe. In 1919, when

Desgrange responded in mid-race to complaints by spectators that they could not tell who was leading, he bestowed a special jersey, a yellow one for the color of his newspaper, on Christophe. He was in that jersey on the next to last stage when, once again, his front fork broke. Again Christophe stopped at a forge and repaired his bicycle and again the lost time cost him his chance for the final victory. He was never to win the Tour.

Another rider who would never win was René Vietto, 'Roi René,' King René, one of the finest French climbers ever. His legend was formed in the 1934 Tour, when he was 20 years old, a former hotel bellboy on the Côte d'Azur who was fulfilling for the first time his dream of riding for France in the Tour. Left far behind in stages over the flat, Vietto stormed into the Alps and Pyrenees, winning three stages and eventually the title of king of the mountains.

In the Pyrenees, Vietto stayed close to his team captain, Antonin Magne, who was being challenged for the yellow jersey by Italian riders. When Magne fell in a descent, Vietto gave him a wheel of his bicycle and waited a few minutes for a team car to get him going again. The next day, on the stage to Luchon, Magne fell on the descent from the Portet d'Aspet and broke his front wheel a second time. Vietto was ahead but, noticing that his leader was not at the front, went back for Magne. When he found him, Vietto continued to follow the rules of the sport and gave Magne his wheel again. Off went Magne, leaving Vietto to wait for the team car. This time it was far behind. When it finally arrived, Vietto was sitting on a stone wall, weeping over his lost chances.

A few days later, Magne won the Tour and Vietto finished fifth, an hour behind. At the end, at the Parc des Princes in Paris, the crowd insisted that the men ride together on the traditional victory circuit. Old timers remember still how glorious Magne looked in the yellow jersey and how Vietto matched him, even if no jersey has ever been — or ever will be — awarded for sacrifice.

1. Right: An advertisement for la Française bicycles shows the route of the first Tour de France, won by Maurice Garin on a la Française. (photo Presse-Sports)

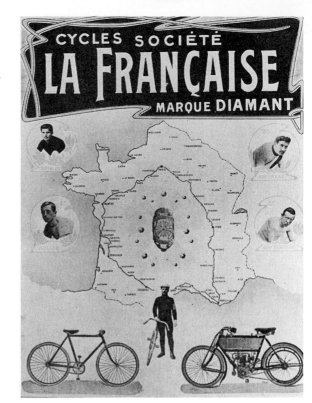

2. Below: The Auberge Reveil Matin in Montgeron as the first Tour started on July 1, 1903. The police escort consisted of two men on horseback, who presumably lost sight of the riders not long after the start. (photo Presse-Sports)

A VIE AU GRAND AIR

ABONNEMENTS	24 Juillet 1903. — N° 254.	PUBLICITÉ
Un an 1* fr.	Rédaction et Admin'stration : 9, Avenue de l'Opéra, PARIS (1er Arrt)	Pages de Couverture, la ligne. La Page. Encartage

MAURICE GARIN, VAINQUEUR DU TOUR DE FRANCE

3. Facing page: Tour winner Maurice Garin was featured on the cover of this French sports magazine dated July 24, 1903. A close look reveals that M. Garin is smoking a cigarette.... (photo Presse-Sports)

4. Right: The plaque at the former Brasserie Zimmer reads, 'Here, on November 20, 1902, it was decided to hold the first Tour de France.' (photo Presse-Sports)

5. Below: Riders in the 1905 Tour sign in for the fifth stage. At left, wearing a Peugeot jersey, is that year's overall winner, Louis Trousellier. (photo Presse-Sports)

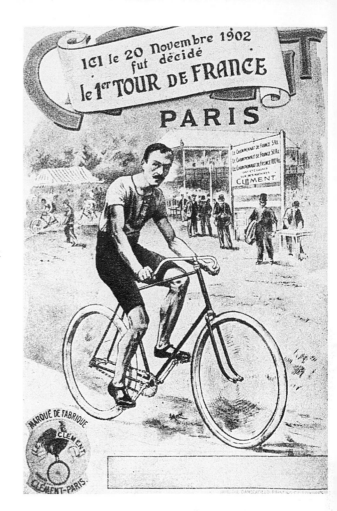

7. Above right: Part of the 1909 pack, 155 strong and by nearly three dozen the largest number of entries so far. (photo Presse-Sports)

6. Above left: René Poittier, the winner in 1906, was also featured on a magazine cover. Note the foot rests on the front fork, for use while descending. (photo Presse-Sports)

8. Below: The pack rolls past French soldiers. Only the two world wars have stopped the race, from 1915 through 1918 and from 1940 through 1946. (photo Presse-Sports)

9. Above: By today's standards, accommodations in 1920 were basic at best. (photo Presse-Sports)

10. Below: Feed zone, 1920 style (photo Presse-Sports)

11. Left: Riders washed up at a horse trough along the road as recently as the 1947 Tour, the first after World War II. (photo Presse-Sports)

12. Below: It was not unusual for Tour riders to fill their water bottles at any convenient well along the route. (photo Presse-Sports)

13. Right:
Six dec-
ades ago,
riders
wore
spare
tires
wrapped
around
their
shoulders
and did
their own
repair
work.
(photo
Presse-
Sports)

14. Below: In the highest mountains of the 1925 Tour, a rider
sometimes had to walk his bike up unpaved roads. (photo
Presse-Sports)

15. Above: At a checkpoint on the Peyresourde climb in the
Pyrenees, riders had to dismount and sign in to prove they had
not cheated by avoiding the peak in the 1927 Tour. (photo
Presse-Sports)

16. Below: The rules say that a rider has to cross the finish line
with his bike, not necessarily on it. (photo Presse-Sports)

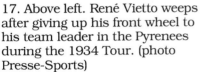

17. Above left. René Vietto weeps after giving up his front wheel to his team leader in the Pyrenees during the 1934 Tour. (photo Presse-Sports)

18. Right: Jacques Goddet lays a wreath at the memorial to Henri Desgrange on the Col du Télégraphe in the Alps. (photo Presse-Sports)

19. Below: The memorial for Tom Simpson on Mont Ventoux, where he died during the 1967 Tour. (photo Billy Stickland)

20. Top left: Bernard
Hinault.

21. Top right: Eddy Merckx.

22. Bottom left: Jacques
Anquetil.

23. Bottom right: Jeannie
Longo after winning the last
Women's Tour de France

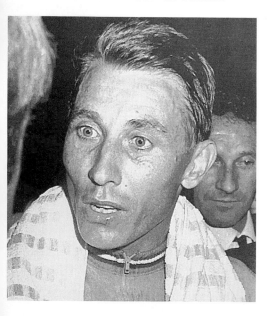

24. Right: A police officer gives the start signal for the first stage using the Tour's own flag. (photo Presse-Sports)

25. Below: The route of the 77th Tour de France (1990)

TOUR 90

Team time trial

Col

Prologue

Rest

ROUEN
5 4.7 301 km
St-Lô
Pont-Audemer
Lisieux
PARIS
Château-Salins
6 6.7 202.5 km Toul **SARREBOURG**
R 5.7

MONT-ST-MICHEL
AVRANCHES
Combourg
Montfort
4 3.7 203 km
Redon
BRÉTIGNY-SUR-ORGE
Dourdan
21 22.7 182.5 km
VITTEL **ÉPINAL**
7 7.7 61.5 km
Amance

NANTES
Bressuire Loudun
3 2.7 228 km
Pouzauges
P 30.6 6.3 km
1 1.7 138.5 km
2 1.7 44.5 km
Gray
8 8.7 181.5 km
BESANÇON
Salins
9 9.7 196 km

FUTUROSCOPE
POITIERS
AUPHELLE (Lac de Vassivière)
Les Rousses
GENEVA
Colombière
Aravis
10 10.7 118.5 km
ST-GERVAIS LE BETTEX

LIMOGES
Châlus
19 20.7 182.5 km
20 21.7 45.5 km
ST-ÉTIENNE
13 14.7 149 km
Croix-de-Chaubouret
FONTAINE (Grenoble)
Albertville
11 11.7 182.5 km
Madeleine
Glandon
Engins
ALPE-D'HUEZ

BORDEAUX
Ribérac
LE PUY Annonay
Romans
VILLARD-DE-LANS

CASTILLON-LA-BATAILLE
Origne
18 19.7 202 km
Captieux
Roquefort
14 15.7 205 km
Saugues
Choizal Mende
12 12.7 33.5 km

MILLAU CAUSSE NOIR
R 13.7

BLAGNAC (Toulouse)
Sié
Lacaune
15 16.7 170 km

PAU
LOURDES
Lombez
Castelnau-Magnoac
REVEL
Castres

17 18.7 150 km
Marie-Blanque
Aubisque
Aspin
Tourmalet
LUZ-ARDIDEN
16 17.7 215 km

26. Right: A despondent Laurent Fignon after his 15th place in the prologue. (photo Presse-Sports)

27. Below: Greg LeMond on his way to second place. (photo Presse-Sports)

28. Above: The pack sets off from high-tech Futuroscope. (photo Presse-Sports)

29. Below: The four breakaways learn from the motorcycle blackboard that their lead on the pack is now 45 seconds. (photo Presse-Sports)

30. Above: At the finish of the first stage, with the lead at 10 minutes and 35 seconds, Frans Maassen signals victory in the sprint. (photo Cor Vos)

31. Below: With Steve Bauer, second from right, in the yellow jersey, 7-Eleven lines up for the team time trial. (photo Presse-Sports)

32. Above: Panasonic riders stay in tight formation during the team time trial. (photo Presse-Sports)

33. Below: But they show signs of disarray near the finish in Futuroscope. Nevertheless, they won the stage. (photo Presse-Sports)

34. Left: A radiant Steve Bauer poses with three props of French life: a beret, a baguette, and the yellow jersey. (photo Presse-Sports)

35. Below: Trees block the road in a protest by farmers over imports and declining incomes. (photo Presse-Sports)

The Respected Anquetil

The names of so many riders live on in the Tour despite accomplishments that are, well, unexceptional. Roger Lapébie, the winner in 1937, had the good fortune to survive into the 1990s and still be present at many stages for introductions and a round of applause. Hugo Koblet, the winner in 1951, owes his fame to his nickname, 'the Pedaler of Charm,' because of his wavy hair and good looks. Jean Robic built his reputation on winning the 1947 Tour, the first after World War II, when the French were hungry for a hero. Jacques Anquetil, the first rider to win four and then five Tours de France, never rivaled them in popularity. His problem was his manner, the long upper lip, the calculating way he was content — not exuberant — with victory.

Asked how he felt about winning a race by 12 seconds, Anquetil replied, "It was 11 more than necessary." A poor boy from Normandy, where his father was first a mason and then a farmer, Anquetil appeared to be aloof and aristocratic to his fellow citizens — what his friends insisted was shyness came across as haughtiness. The adjectives usually applied to him were 'cool and distant.' In a sport founded on asceticism, Anquetil liked the company of women and sometimes for dinner during a race he appreciated a lobster and a glass, or even a bottle, of champagne.

Many of the French resented Anquetil's style, preferring their idols to be a simpler sort, even if they were not winners. In Anquetil's case, most Frenchmen preferred his longtime rival Raymond Poulidor, the eternal also-ran, three times second in the Tour, five times third, and never first. Smiling, humble and beaten, Poulidor was the people's choice, Anquetil merely respected. He died bravely, refusing to acknowledge his stomach cancer, in 1987 at the age of 53. Although he stopped racing in 1969, Anquetil never strayed far. Only four months before his death he remained a television commentator during the Tour. In addition he was the head official for the Paris–Nice race and a selector of French teams for the world championships.

A consummate time trialer, Anquetil dominated the Tour in the early 1960s, winning from 1961 through 1964 to go with his victory in his debut in 1957. He also won the Vuelta de España in 1963 and the Giro in 1960 and 1964, becoming the first rider to triumph in each of the three great Tours. Anquetil was far less successful in the classics — except for the Grand Prix des Nations, a long time trial, which he captured nine times.

No feat earned him adoration. Respect, but not love, was his due even after he won the Dauphiné Libéré stage race in 1965, ate a hasty dinner, flew across country to Bordeaux and won the 600-kilometer Bordeaux–Paris race that night and the next day. The French, charged Bernard Hinault, another five-time winner of the Tour, could not tolerate winners because they themselves were not.

The Revered Merckx

Eddy Merckx was 24 years old and riding in his first Tour de France in 1969 when he served notice that he had become 'the Cannibal,' hungry for all victories. Two years before, he had won the world championship, so the Belgian was known, but not until this day was he feared.

On a stage in the Pyrenees from Luchon to Mourenx Ville Nouvelle through 'the circle of death,' Merckx was at the front over the first two climbs, the Peyresourde and the Aspin Passes. Two hundred meters from the top of the third climb, the giant Tourmalet, he left the pack behind, jumping away from his teammate Martin Van den Bossche and from two rivals, Roger Pingeon and Raymond Poulidor. Down the descent Merckx sped, opening a lead of 25 seconds.

His Faema team car drew level with him and his coach, Guillaume Driessens, warned, "Watch yourself. The finish is a long way off and you still have to climb the Aubisque." Soon his lead was up to 55 seconds and by the foot of the Aubisque it reached 1:15. At the summit, with 70 kilometers ahead until the finish, Merckx was a stunning 7:55 free. The rest of the way was flat or downhill and 56 kilometers from the end the lead stood at 8:05. Starting to feel the ordeal in his legs, he weakened somewhat before coasting in a winner by 7:56. There were six stages to go but Merckx had just won the first of his five Tours.

Why had he gone off that way? "I attacked on the Tourmalet because I felt so disappointed," he said. "Van den Bossche, my teammate, really wanted to pass first over the mountain. But he told me two days before that he was leaving the team next year. I didn't like hearing that, especially in the middle of the Tour. So I was disappointed, even angry. I attacked on the Tourmalet so that I would be first over, not he."

That was Merckx at the start of his Tour career. Five years later he had won four more Tours — 1970, '71, '72 and '74 — and nearly every other honor in the sport. The world championship? In 1967, '71 and '74. The Giro? In 1968, '70, '72, '73 and '74. The Vuelta? In 1973. The Tour of Switzerland? In 1974. Paris–Nice? In 1969, '70 and '71. Paris–Roubaix? In 1968, '70 and '73. Milan–San Remo? In 1966, '67, '69, '71, '72, '75 and '76. The Tour of Lombardy? In 1971 and '72. The Tour of Flanders? In 1969 and '75. Liège–Bastogne–Liège? In 1969, '71, '72, '73 and '75. Amstel Gold Race? In 1973 and '75. He tacked on the world record for the hour's ride against the clock in 1972.

To the general public, one of his greatest victories occurred in one of the two Tours he entered that he did not win. Fracturing a cheekbone in a fall during the 1975 Tour, Merckx gamely continued to chase after Bernard Thévenet, the Frenchman who was in the yellow jersey. The Tour's doctors recommended that the Belgian quit and go home for treatment, but he insisted on staying in the race for the final five stages.

"If I had not finished this race, Thévenet's victory would not have looked as great as it is," he said finally in Paris, where he finished second by 2:47. In defeat, the Cannibal had turned gracious.

Chapter 4
_____ The Tour's Business

A small, exceedingly small, news item in _l'Équipe_ late in the fall of 1990 reported that _l'affaire Félix Lévitan_ had been settled to everybody's satisfaction and that no further legal proceedings were foreseen. End of item.

If the Tour de France is a pocket kingdom, Lévitan was its monarch. For decades he governed his subjects with an austere benevolence, crackling orders over _Radio Tour_ from the limousine in which he ruled over each day's stage with Jacques Goddet, his co-director. Courteous yet sardonic, authoritarian and nearly humorless, Lévitan was asked once to explain the division of powers between himself and Goddet. "It's easy," Lévitan replied. "I'm in charge."

A Monarch Disposed

Then, at the age of 76, he was overthrown. Lévitan arrived at his office one morning in the spring of 1987 to find the lock on his door changed and a French court official waiting with a search warrant to poke through files and desk drawers. The official came up with a letter that seemed to confirm what an audit of the Tour's books had hinted at: As managing agent of the Société du Tour de France, the organizers and owners of the race, Levitan secretly used corporate funds to cover a huge deficit of the 1983 Tour of America.

While countercharge followed charge and threats of law-suits fouled the air, the public got a rare look at the financial affairs of the bicycle race. The Tour de France is a sport, but the Société du Tour de France is a business, as it made clear in publicly firing Lévitan, challenging "the reality of his management."

That one hurt, Levitan said.

Nobody had challenged his management since he joined

Tour officialdom in 1947 for the first postwar race. That year, two Paris newspapers, *Parisien Libéré*, now a splashy tabloid without the 'Libéré' in its name, and *l'Équipe* became co-sponsors of the Tour. *L'Équipe*, where Goddet was editor, dominated the sponsoring organization by virtue of his role alone at the helm since 1936 and the paper's roots in Henri Desgrange's *l'Auto*. *Parisien Libéré*, where Lévitan rose from cycling correspondent to editor, was a distant second.

Nevertheless he began to climb the ladder. In 1962 he became Goddet's deputy and in 1978 his equal; when Goddet informally retired in 1987 at the age of 81, Lévitan was expected to remain in charge. Their relations were never plain, but Goddet was considered the inspirational force, the thunderer in his daily column in *l'Équipe* during the race, and Levitan merely the manager.

He managed well, Lévitan insisted after his firing, when he went before a hall packed with reporters ('my peers,' he called them) and opened the books. Until 1974, he revealed, the race ran in the red each year. In the next decade, the Tour was in the black by nearly $3 million. Look, he continued, the budget for the 1987 Tour was $2.5 million, with $1.5 million to be paid by West Berlin for the honor of being host to the start.

Lévitan slid off the incriminating letter about the Tour of America deficit, which was put at $549,000 plus interest and other fees — a total of $839,000. Officially the Tour de France had little to do with the ill-fated three-day race through Virginia into Washington; its sole connection with the one-shot race was letting Lévitan act as 'technical consultant.' Unofficially, secretly, Lévitan gave a $500,000 write-off to the Tour of America organizers, Broadcasting Rights International Corp., the French company that also negotiated the sale of the Tour de France's U.S. television rights to CBS. Instead of retaining 30 percent of the fee as its commission, Broadcasting Rights was allowed to keep most of CBS's estimated $350,000 annual payments in 1985 and '86. The company had turned over to the Société du Tour de France $85,000 in 1985 and $50,000 in 1986, but was scheduled to pay $280,000 in 1987, Lévitan insisted.

Had he benefited personally from this arrangement? Scornfully, Lévitan denied that. "Here's what I'm worth: I inherited nothing. When I got back from the war, I didn't own even a pair of sheets. And I went back to being a newspaperman, badly paid at first, better off later." He produced a photostat of his latest pay slip from *Parisien Libéré* to show that his salary was earned as its semi-retired editor and not as its man running the Tour de France. For that, he continued, he was paid nothing. All he owned, he said, were the apartment in Cannes where he lived most of the week, a home in the country, a café in a small town where he was once mayor and a mobile home parked at a vacation campsite. If his private lifestyle was not extravagant, his public one was spartan: a small, inelegant office where he often lunched on a ham sandwich, a glass of water and a coffee, while directing a fulltime staff of 40.

Now he was gone, he acknowledged. An amiable settlement was always possible but, if not, he would sue for nearly $1 million. "I want much more than money, however. They must return my honor."

To some, he hadn't lost much of it. Lévitan soaked up the Tour of America debt in a possibly illegal and certainly arrogant attempt to do the right thing, as he saw it — to further the cause of international bicycle racing.

Despite his role as the tactician, the manager, Lévitan had been the visionary. While others resisted, Lévitan insisted on introducing the Women's Tour de France in 1984; two years after he was gone, so was it. When Goddet called in 1982 for a return to national teams every four years to vary the mix, Lévitan pushed instead for the Tour de France to welcome amateur teams. He won and the Colombians arrived in 1983. Lévitan dreamed of a start some year in Japan or the United States, of teams entering from Eastern Europe. He arranged starts in West Berlin, in Frankfurt, in Basel, and he toyed with the idea of a stage or two in Moscow or Warsaw.

Bringing in the Americans was another pet project. In 1980 he floated plans for a Tour of Florida, in 1981 for a Tour of California. When the race in Virginia was announced in 1982,

Lévitan jumped in. "I am merely a consultant," he explained deprecatingly. "I am the doctor called in for a second opinion, except that in this case nobody is sick."

In the end, the Société du Tour de France decided otherwise.

As the writer Terry Pratchett has noted, "A kingdom is made up of all sorts of things. Ideas. Loyalties. Memories. It all sort of exists together. And then all these things create some kind of life. Not a body kind of life, more like a living idea." Lévitan and Goddet were not easy men to replace.

A View From the Inside

At the age of 85 in 1990, Jacques Goddet missed his first Tour de France in more than a half century and spent the opening week instead at Wimbledon, watching the tennis championships there. When he returned, with the Tour in its second week, he followed the race through television and the newspapers. "It's interesting to see it from the outside after so many years on the inside," he said in an interview late in the fall. "I'm like the average fan now."

That was a sinister thought, although Goddet hadn't meant it that way. The truth was that, although the Tour's exposure was higher than ever because of increased television coverage, the crowds at the side of the road were noticeably declining. Like Goddet himself, the average fan seemed now to prefer tennis, or soccer during the World Cup every four years. Even *l'Équipe* gave over its front page to the World Cup in Italy during the first week of the Tour, relegating the bicycle race to somewhere beyond Page 12. The Tour emerged only when Wimbledon and the World Cup ended.

Goddet was working on his memoirs. They would concentrate more on his years as editor of *l'Équipe* than his years with the Tour, he explained, because he felt that so little was known about the newspaper and so much about the race. Nevertheless, the questions he was asked in the interview all had to do with the Tour, and he answered willingly.

Question: How would you compare today's Tour to those in the 1930s?

Answer: On the sporting level, the organizers have provided so many improvements now: better means of taking care of the riders, better food and water, better lodging, better help during the race. We've given it a high-technology character that is adapted to our times. Even the roads have become totally different. All this is a plus. Everything has become not easier, but more orderly.

We've removed a lot of the inhuman character, which I admit the sport owes a lot of its reputation to but which is not in the spirit of these days.

Of course, this means that the racers are more equal. And teams are much better organized than they used to be. It's very hard, for example, to break away from a pack that is moving at 50 kilometers an hour. So there's a danger of losing that sense of adventure, that opportunity for an exploit, that is so necessary to the sport.

Q: Overall, have these changes been for the better or the worse?

A: What has changed has been for the better. Maybe what is for the worse is that more things have not changed.

Q: Do you think that cycling is less popular now as a spectator sport than it was in the 1930s or 1950s?

A: In the sense that 'popular' means 'that which interests a large public,' it's more popular now because it reaches a vaster public than in the '30s because of television coverage around the world.

Q: Doesn't the average person seem less attracted these days to the ideals of sacrifice and suffering that are so much a part of bicycle racing?

A: They want security. The whole world has become much more interested in security. There is so much misery in this world that everybody looks for peace and quiet, definitely.

And the Tour especially refuses security. It involves and needs the concept of facing pain and defeat. Sacrifice is partly responsible for the Tour's popularity. Sacrifice is part of cycling's legend, certainly part of the Tour's legend.

40

I'm not saying that personally I would like the riders to encounter huge difficulties, but it is necessary for the sport.

Q: Is there still much sacrifice and suffering in the Tour?

A: Less than before because we've humanized cycling. Everything is better. There is still some immense suffering, such as in the Giro when a stage has to be run in a snowstorm or in Paris–Roubaix on the cobblestones, of course. But the romantic norm had become too pronounced in the Tour.

Q: The huge amount of money available now is different than in your day, isn't it?

A: It's different. The arrival of money from television and sponsors, the increase in fees for stage towns have allowed a prize list that is finally worthy of the race and the racers. That's a good thing. And essential.

Of course, we must be careful. Money is always a dangerous thing because it can change so much. But it's unavoidable and necessary.

Q: What about complaints that the sport itself has become too materialistic?

A: Well, the teams are much more professional than they used to be. Really big companies, multinationals, invest in the teams. The sport has become more serious, more structured, perhaps more permanent. But we have to be careful that these sponsors don't try to change the form of the sport. Bicycle racing must be protected.

Q: The Tour seems to be getting easier, doesn't it, with fewer days in the high mountains?

A: My personal belief, and a longtime one, is that, while we must honor the mountains, the Tour cannot be a struggle only among the best climbers. That isn't fair to the others. We all know of some fantastic racers who could never play an important part in the Tour because their body types did not allow them to climb well.

I've always said that the Tour de France has to be a more complete test than just mountains. They will remain an essential element — but not the only one. The dominance of the mountains must be softened a bit.

Q: That happened this year and will be even more noticeable in 1991. What other changes do you hope to see?

A: When we added time trials, they were a big correction to the imbalance. Next I'm all for giving sprinters and riders on the flat some rights.

We have 8 or 10 stages in each Tour that have no real value. There's no use in simply doing kilometer after kilometer, burning out climbers like the Colombians. It's not reasonable. I think we are too attached to the classic forms of bicycle racing. Maybe I just didn't have the courage to stand up and speak out against this. It has to change.

Why not short stages, 60-kilometer stages? There are short, steep hills all over France. If we added hills like that before the finish of a short stage, it would not necessarily help only climbers.

Q: Will national teams ever return to the Tour?

A: I think that will be very difficult. Trade teams have a strength, a permanence. They invest a lot of money and they would not accept being excluded from the Tour, the high point of the season. That's certain. And it wouldn't really be fair to them.

But why not national teams every four years, say? The season could be rearranged to make the Giro or the Vuelta the high point for trade teams and the Tour the high point for national teams.

There would be problems, of course. Major racers from the same country are rivals, the biggest rivals, and it's extremely difficult to get them to cooperate. We see that in the world championship. And that's just one stage, while the Tour has 22.

But a Tour de France with national teams would be very beautiful, on paper at least, because there are so many new countries in the sport.

Q: What is your fondest memory of all your years with the Tour?

A: Oh, I have so many it's unfair to choose one.

Q: What do you admire most about the sport?

A: What is so great about bicycle racing is the respect it teaches the riders to have for their bodies. The body feeds the brain. That's why I love the sport.

Q: The greatest racer you saw?

A: Merckx was the greatest. In everything.

Q: Much greater than Hinault?

A: Yes. Hinault had great strengths but he didn't take advantage of all his possibilities. He had his own ideas, like not appreciating Paris–Roubaix. He took one seriously and won it. He could have won Paris–Roubaix many times. It's a race that permits great champions to demonstrate their greatness.

Q: Are there still Giants of the Road?

A: Yes. Hinault was one, LeMond could be considered one or very close to one. He really is a hero, partly because of his accident — it's very romantic. A hero is somebody who has known adversity and pain. Bicycle racing needs heroism.

The New Rulers

Over two years following Lévitan's involuntary abdication, the Société du Tour de France was to go through three chief organizers before dividing the job between Jean-Pierre Carenso, who had spent his career with advertising companies, and Jean-Marie Leblanc, the respected editor of *Vélo* magazine and a bicycling reporter for *l'Équipe*. Carenso handles the business side and Leblanc, also a former rider who participated in the 1968 and 1970 Tours, directs operations out on the road.

Both have been successful in ways even Goddet and Lévitan could not have imagined. As a former rider and journalist, Leblanc is admirably sensitive to the needs of reporters and the racing pack. He is willing to admit mistakes, and does not makes them twice. His tone is reasonable and conciliatory.

Deep in the background, the businessman matched him.

If, only a dozen years before, the Tour de France was barely in the black, that, as they say, was then: an era of limited television coverage and modest sponsoring and advertising fees. And this is now: The race had become so big a money machine that reporters joked about its very name. 'The Tour d'Argent,' one publication subtitled the race this year. 'The Tour de Franc,' said another.

Both acknowledged, of course, that vast sums of money are needed to power what is virtually a sovereign state, complete with its own motorcycle police force (members of the Garde Républicaine from Paris), its own traveling bank (the only one in France allowed to remain open on Bastille Day) and more than 3,500 subjects (the 198 riders who start each year are far outnumbered by the 660 reporters and photographers, 264 team officials, mechanics and masseurs, 745 chauffeurs and technical assistants, 20 judges, 263 race officials and employees and 1,360 sponsors' pitchmen).

The money also provides prizes twice as big as any other race's. The Giro d'Italia and the Vuelta de España are just as long as the Tour's three weeks and almost as demanding on the riders' ability to suffer and triumph in the mountains, but neither comes close to matching the Tour's prize list. The 1990 winner was to receive a check for 2 million French francs (then $363,000), just part of the 10 million francs shared by the riders. In 1987, prize money barely topped 6 million francs and in 1989 it totaled 8 million.

Where does the money come from? The $75,000 that each of the 22 teams puts up as an entry fee doesn't cover much more than its hotels and meals. A significant part of revenue is paid by the municipalities that welcome the arrival or departure of the Tour on each stage. The 1990 Tour began in Futuroscope, for example. Not many people had previously heard of Futuroscope, which is why the computer theme park near Poitiers in western France was willing to pay close to $1 million to play host. For three days, Futuroscope was the dateline of newspaper stories and the background for live television coverage to dozens of countries. Eurovision was there and so was ABC from the United States, NHK from Japan and a handful of radio networks from Colombia. In all, the municipalities furnished 15 percent of the Tour's 1990 income of 100 million francs — an increase of 10 percent from

1989.

A much bigger slice of income came from sponsors (65 to 70 percent) including such corporate heavyweights as Fiat, Panasonic, Coca-Cola and the Crédit Lyonnais bank, all with three-year contracts costing between 12 and 18 million francs each. Smaller fees were paid by secondary sponsors and by the 22 advertisers in 489 vehicles in the publicity caravan. The rest accrued from television rights (20 to 25 percent), where fees have doubled in two years. Not a centime or a sou came from admission fees — although 15 to 20 million fans observe the race live, they watch free of charge.

Of the 100 million francs' income, 90 million was spent on the race, with nearly 90 percent of that going for such fixed fees as teams' meals, hotels, and police protection along all the roads, plus salaries of the organizers' 46 permanent and 217 parttime employees. That left 10 million francs for profit. Lévitan might have been stunned by such figures. Without really changing at all, the Tour had grown in so many ways in the three years since he had been forced out. Then, Greg LeMond had set a salary standard by winning a $1-million contract over three years with La Vie Claire. Now LeMond was making nearly $2 million for the year and a platoon of others were nearing $1 million annually.

The old-timers complained that the pack thought of nothing but money. Bernard Thévenet, twice a winner of the Tour de France in the 1970s, spoke for the old school: "For our generation, cycling was a way upward. We were more motivated to make the sacrifices cycling demands. Money came later. Now it seems that some riders want everything at once. That's impossible."

Chapter 5
___ Roads Leading to the Tour

"Vanishing France" a friend has titled his book. He tells of the disappearance of the horse-drawn canal barge, of the ripsawing of hundreds of chestnut trees for a highway along the Seine in Paris, of the burial of the bean fields of Arpajon under highrise housing. "Tourists visiting Cognac used to detour through the village of Baignes to admire its medieval covered markets," he writes. "To provide them with parking space, the village fathers tore down the markets. Now there is plenty of space, but no tourists." The book was written in 1975 and much more has vanished since.

To be fair, much remains. "Plus ça change, plus c'est la même chose," the French like to say — the more things change, the more they're the same. The Tour de France is a fine example. For all its computers and marketing programs, it remains simply a bicycle race that pits one man against another and both against fatigue, the weather and the laws of chance. "You can't lose a bicycle race," the American rider Andy Hampsten likes to say. "There can be one winner, but not 150 losers."

Suffering, sacrifice and dedication in the small world of bicycle racing are not unique to the Tour de France, of course. They are also found along the roads leading to the Tour.

Center of the World

All does not go well for professional bicycle racing in its stronghold, *la France profonde* — deep France, vanishing France. In the desolate North, the 1990 Tour de France passed only by plane as it traveled from Normandy to the Moselle. In Chambéry, hundreds of thousands of dollars in receipts from the 1989 world championships are still missing. And in Bessèges, a heart was broken.

Not that a casual visitor could tell that there are troubles in Bessèges. Sheltered in a long valley along the Cèze River in the Cévennes mountains of south-central France, the village has much to be pleased with. Its old stone houses are well kept, even lovely when the forsythia in so many yards bursts from brown into yellow.

The boom days of coal mining are long over, but trade life remains active along Bessèges's main street, the Rue Albert Chambonnet (*résistante* and martyr, 1903–1944.) At the right time of day the street's bars and butchers, its groceries and banks are packed. Across the river sits the factory of AI Industry, a maker of electric-current regulators and employer of some of Bessèges's nearly 4,500 inhabitants. Not far away is the railroad station, where seven trains a day arrive from the outside world, mainly Alès, 30 kilometers away. Life here is uneventful.

"Let's face it," said Roland Fangille, "Bessèges is a little provincial town. It is what it is. Nothing more."

Yet once a year Fangille helps make Bessèges something much more: the center of the professional cycling world. For 20 years he has organized l'Étoile de Bessèges, a five-day series of races that he characterizes as "the first big rendez-vous of the season."

Starting the nine-month season in early February, the major teams have long appeared in the Étoile de Bessèges to begin training for the big races of spring and summer. "We've had Fignon, Hinault, Zoetemelk," Fangille said. "We had LeMond when he was just beginning. Raymond Poulidor rode in the first Étoile de Bessèges. We represent something."

Short and stocky, his cheeks ruddy, Fangille speaks excitedly in the strong accent of the Gard region. "I once was a rider, I rode with Anquetil and Poulidor," he boasted. "I almost became a professional. I had some offers from the Ford team." By then he was too old and, at 30, stopped racing to enter the furniture business and organize the first Étoile. He has been at it ever since and, like the five other volunteers he has cajoled into joining his organizing committee, he has never made a centime.

"No one is paid," he said. "The time when we'll be paid is still to come. We do it for the sport."

Fangille, then, is a lover. But for many months he was a rejected lover; worse, a lover rejected publicly. During the 1990 Étoile de Bessèges, most of the riders lost interest and simply stopped in the middle of a daily stage. Only 19 riders carried on the Étoile as, half an hour behind their breakaway, more than 130 men realized they would never catch up and they might as well quit. Imagine Fangille's humiliation when the riders showed Bessèges and the world how little his beloved race meant.

Remembering that moment, Fangille grows more excited. It does not help him to know that even in the Tour de France stages have sometimes been stopped by riders to protest safety conditions or drug tests or long transfers by car or bus from the end of one day's race to the start of the next.

What was there to protest in the Étoile de Bessèges?

"Nothing," Fangille said strongly.

Once the riders stopped and dispersed to their hotels, nobody else could explain it either. Nothing had been prearranged, nobody had planned to shame the organizers.

"We never learned what really happened," Fangille said. "Even the riders, nobody knows what really happened. The race was very fast, since the first two hours were ridden at 45 kilometers an hour. I've read that some riders complained that it was a Tour de France stage they were given in February. Also, out of 15 teams in the race, 9 had riders in the breakaway. So at the back, what do you think they cared about?"

Fangille shook his head at the thought of his wasted work and squandered budget. To conform to rules of the International Federation of Professional Cycling, he had raised his spending in three years from 800,000 francs to 1.8 million. The Gard region, Bessèges and the surrounding villages through which the race passes supply most of his funds.

"It costs a lot of money to organize a race," he said. "The federation lays down strict rules about the prizes, which have to be logical. Then we have the cost of hotels, police, doctors.

We have to clean up afterward. We have a photo finish. We give out 300,000, 350,000 francs in prizes. It's expensive but, well, logical."

Understandably, Fangille was near tears when international officials reinstated the racers who had quit, merely debiting them with the time they were behind. Nobody could recall a precedent for reinstating riders who had called off their race. In Fangille's eyes, punishment was demanded and he decreed it.

The Étoile de Bessèges, he announced, had been run for the final time. The 20th edition was the last. Let the riders mock another organizer, as he predicted might well happen. "The problem we had can happen again tomorrow or the day after," he said.

In Bessèges, Fangille is known for settling all of his race's bills within a week of the finish. "Why do I need any problems?" he asked. He paid the bills this time too, and the more hours he spent closing out the race, the more he realized how much it meant to him. So, a month later, he changed his mind. Like most lovers, he is willing to forgive if not forget.

"There will be another Étoile," he said. "When I met afterward with the team managers, everyone told me, 'We have nothing against the organization or the race.' No one understood.

"The people of Bessèges support me. The race must continue. We definitely represent something."

Occupational Hazards

Nearly everybody in the small world of professional bicycle racing remembers the photograph, and Davis Phinney remembers it best. It shows him sitting on the ground behind a car, his right hand up to his face, his body limp and blood everywhere.

"I just center-punched that car," Phinney said. Traveling at high speed and with his head down in the 1988 Liège–Bastogne–Liège race, he rammed the stopped car from the rear and went head-first into the window, which shattered. "I just had time to get my left arm up to my face," the American rider said, repeating the motion and showing a long scar on the underside of his arm. "I lost the use of my little finger. It just hangs there, limp."

His nose was broken and his face so badly ripped that he needed 150 stitches to repair the damage. The scars have faded now. When he laughs, which is often, the scars around his eyes blend into a worldly crinkle. "People say they add character to my face," Phinney boasted.

Liège–Bastogne–Liège is even older than the Tour de France. Begun in 1890 as a race for amateurs, it is generally regarded as the oldest of bicycle racing's classic, or one-day, races by one year over Bordeaux–Paris. Some historians of the sport point out, however, that it did not become a race for professionals — the usual yardstick for measuring a race's longevity — until 1894 and then resumed its amateur status until 1912.

That amateur tradition lingers. Until 1990, Liège–Bastogne–Liège was organized by the 'Royal Cyclist's Pesant Club Liègeois,' which proudly listed on its stationery such local sponsors as a furniture manufacturer and a pinball-machine supplier. In a way it was charming to have a mom and pop organization running such an important race in an era when marketing studies and computer printouts are beginning to dominate the sport. Sometimes Liège–Bastogne–Liège seemed more like an overgrown *kermesse*, one of the lots-of-fun-for-the-family races that nearly every town in Belgium holds annually. Sometimes, though, because it was all so casual and the weather often rainy and even snowy, Liège–Bastogne–Liège was unsafe. Roads up and down some of its hills were narrow and clogged with spectators, making it difficult for the racers to get through. Press photographers on motorcycles were allowed to shadow the riders so closely that they could block a breakaway.

In 1988, before Phinney was hurt, dozens of riders spilled into a drainage trench that had been dug across the course. In major races, the organizers monitor the roads beforehand to prevent unexpected obstacles or they post sentries with yellow flags to warn the riders, but in Liège–Bastogne–Liège nobody seemed to know about the trench. "I was in that crash," Phinney said, "and I wrecked both wheels. By the time I got going again, I was five minutes down and ready to quit." Mike Neel, then the manager of the 7-Eleven team, drove up and told Phinney and a teammate, Alex Stieda, to stay in the race.

" 'Come on, let's go,' he said," Phinney remembered. "I was feeling so good that we just took off. Because of the crash, there were riders all strung out ahead and I was raging and went by these groups. I was going, going, going. Team cars were all along the road and I tried to ride in the center, passing between the cars. I was leapfrogging cars but getting tired because I had been chasing for about 10 kilometers. I could see the pack and they were about 200 meters away, so I just put my head down and rode.

"I heard horns honking behind me and I thought it was just team cars wanting riders to move over and I put my head up and a car had just stopped in the middle of the road."

The car belonged to the Isoglass team and had stopped to replace a punctured tire for one of its riders. At the time, Phinney estimated, he was racing at 50 kilometers an hour and the car was about 5 feet ahead of him.

"It was a pretty narrow road," he continued, "but he didn't stop on the side, the way you're supposed to. He stopped in the middle and I plowed into him. It was my fault. You assume there'll be nothing there, that the race is ongoing, but ultimately everything is pretty much your fault in bike racing."

He was rushed by ambulance to Liège for a two-hour operation. Two days later he was back on his bicycle, riding it on rollers, as racers do to warm up. "Mostly it was to sweat and clean out the anesthetics from my body," he said. A few days more and he was riding through the streets, careful about the cast on his left arm. "Like a batter who has been hit by a pitch, the trick is to get going right away, not brood about it." Ten days after he left the hospital he entered his first race, a *kermesse* in Belgium. Four weeks to the day after the crash, Phinney outsprinted the pack to win a stage of the Tour of Romandie, a Swiss race.

Phinney returned to Liège–Bastogne–Liège in 1989.

"I was really uptight and the closer I got to where I had crashed, I started to get this block in my mind. I couldn't ride in the field with everybody else. I was so tense that I was riding last guy. Once we went past the point, I started to relax."

Because he had been riding in Europe since the earliest race in February and because he was still recovering from a tendon operation on his left knee months before, the 7-Eleven team sent him home to Boulder, Colorado, a week before the 1990 Liège–Bastogne–Liège. "I'm really glad to miss that," he said.

The race is now one of the 12 classics that compose the prestigious and lucrative World Cup. As such, its organizers were persuaded to bring in outside advisers and they asked the Société du Tour de France to help map a safer course and control the crowds and media motorcycles. The Tour de France people recommended eliminating one hill as too dangerous and adding three, for a total of 10.

As black clouds scudded across the sky, 196 riders started the 256-kilometer race south into the Ardennes and back to Liège. "It's very difficult and very hilly, quite a change from the first classics," explained Steve Bauer, a Canadian and Phinney's teammate with 7-Eleven. "The Tour of Flanders has hills but they're short. In Liège–Bastogne–Liège, you need more stamina, more endurance. You need good climbing ability. You've been riding flat and riding cobblestones and you're not really prepared to be riding up and down. That's a tough transition."

This was a typical Liège–Bastogne–Liège. The hills were as long as ever and the weather — frequently hard and cold rain as the riders passed the spruce forests of southeastern Belgium — as bad as ever. With 22 kilometers to go, Eric Van Lancker of Panasonic broke away before the final climb. Of the 136 riders who finished, only two — Jean-Claude Leclercq of Helvetia and Steven Rooks of Panasonic — had the strength

52

to go after him and Rooks was doing it as a piece of strategy, to put Leclercq in a nutcracker between two teammates.

Van Lancker crossed the finish line 34 seconds clear to give Belgium its first victory in the classic since 1978. The two others began to sprint for second place, with Leclercq coming straight down the middle and Rooks out to his left. The road should have been clear for Rooks but just behind the finish line a long line of photographers, reporters, officials and simple onlookers jutted directly into his path. Luckily Rooks was racing with his head up and spotted them. He swerved away, losing ground as Leclercq crossed the line ahead of him. Nobody was hurt.

It was difficult not to think then about Phinney, an acclaimed sprinter, the best in America and one of the best in the world. With a big laugh, he tells about the attendant at a ski lift who did a double-take when he saw his scarred face.

"He asked, 'What happened? A cat scratch you?'

" 'Yeah,' I said. 'And you know what kind of cat it was? A jaguar.' "

Hard Luck Tale

Rudy Dhaenens does not fool himself about his slight gifts and limited ambition as a professional racer. "Laurent Fignon wins more than I do, probably because he expects more of himself," Dhaenens said of the rider then ranked No. 1 in computerized standings of the world's leading 600 professionals. Entering April, with the Tour de France three months off, Dhaenens ranked No. 169.

The problem is not only talent but also luck. Nobody should know as much about bad luck as Rudy Dhaenens does.

There was the stage in the 1989 Tour, for example, when he broke away alone and had the race won until the final curve, 400 or 500 meters from the finish line. "I took the corner too fast, maybe, or something happened with my wheel, maybe, and I slipped," he recalled. "I still don't know."

His bicycle went out from under him and he was thrown to the road. By the time he got to his feet and found that his rear wheel was mangled, he could only scream in rage as the rest of the pack shot by. From an easy winner, Dhaenens became the last man across the line. It doesn't happen often.

"It just happened, so what can you do?" he asked quietly as he lounged in his motel room, awaiting the Paris–Roubaix race. "It just happened, it just happened," he repeated.

Victories come rarely to the 30-year-old Dhaenens, a Belgian with the PDM team, and when they do, they are not often as prestigious as in the Tour. "In a race like the Tour de France, I can't hope to win every day," he acknowledged. "When you're a Fignon or a LeMond, a superman, you have all those days when you can win: the mountains, the time trials. But when you're a normal rider, you have maybe 12 days in the Tour de France when you can win." In fact, until then the major victory of his seven-year career was in a stage of the 1986 Tour.

The personable and hard-working Dhaenens had come close in other races, including fourth place in the Het Volk in 1988, seventh in Milan–San Remo in 1989, third in the Belgian national championship in 1985 and second in Paris-Roubaix in 1986. He nearly won the 1990 Tour of Flanders, finally finishing second in a two-man breakaway with Moreno Argentin, a renowned sprinter and former world champion in the professional road race. "It was a good day for me," Dhaenens said. "I was riding well, in good condition. But I didn't have luck and had a fast sprinter with me. It would have been better to be with a Fignon or somebody like that, somebody I could beat in the sprint. But I was with Argentin and had nowhere to go."

The result was predictable.

The Tour of Flanders victory was a major one for Argentin, 30, who has been struggling in the last few years but still manages annually to win a few small races plus a classic — Liège–Bastogne–Liège in 1985, '86 and '87 — or the Italian national championship in 1983 and 1989.

"There are guys who aren't often good during the year but

when they're good, they win," Dhaenens explained. "Like Argentin: when he's super, he wins. He's super maybe four or five days a year, but he wins four of the five times.

"I'm not like him. I'm always in the top group, usually in the front, but never win. And that's what's important in bicycle races."

Dhaenens was hopeful about Paris–Roubaix, which is known as the queen of classics because of its age (first run in 1896), its distinguished list of winners (Coppi, Bobet, Merckx, de Vlaeminck, Moser, Hinault, Kelly) and its difficulty. Run over 265 kilometers of flat land between Compiègne, north of Paris, and Roubaix, the race includes 57 kilometers of cobblestones on stretches along country roads and through a forest. These cobblestones, some of them huge and irregularly aligned, bounce the riders so roughly that aches and pains last for a week afterward. Paris–Roubaix is nicknamed 'the hell of the north' because of its cobblestones and their setting in dirt roads. When they are wet, they cause spills; when they are dry, the first riders leave a trail of dust that chokes those behind. Punctures are commonplace.

"It's a lot of pain and misery but it's like a heavyweight championship fight," said Michael Wilson, an Australian rider with Helvetia. "You know you're going to get beaten up but without that beating, you're not going to make the big money. So you've got to do it."

Dhaenens usually does well in the race, because it demands the concentration he offers in place of talent. He dreams of winning Paris–Roubaix and has come close. In addition to his second place in 1986, he was third in 1987 and fifth in 1985. Those years he primarily assisted his team leader, but in 1990 he had a rare chance to be the PDM leader, replacing Sean Kelly, who broke his right collarbone in a crash in the Tour of Flanders.

"I'm happy with that role because I feel the guys believe in me," Dhaenens said. "I'm on the other side now. We always have good riders on the team and they have the best potential for winning. Plus me, I'm not the winning type. So I did it for them and now the guys will do it for me."

He understood the tactics to be followed. "You need to stay in the front because of the crashes, narrow roads and side winds. You have to be ready for a long race. In the other classics, the real start is later; in the Tour of Flanders, I start really riding after 160 kilometers, so the race begins with 100 kilometers to go. Here, after 90 kilometers, you hit the cobblestones and the race starts. And there are 160 kilometers to go.

"To win, you need luck. There are so many good riders in a race like Paris–Roubaix that the winner needs to be lucky."

Up to a point, Dhaenens had luck in the race the next day. He stormed through the cobblestoned sectors near the front of the pack, managing to avoid most of the dust on a dry and windswept day, and dodged the riders on the ground in front of him. In the feared Arenberg section of the worst cobblestones, Dhaenens was able to keep his bicycle under him, its tires unpunctured. As late in the race as Wattiessart, with 50 kilometers and 7 stretches of cobblestones to go, Dhaenens was still with the main group of riders who were chasing three breakaways. The gap narrowed to 40 seconds and a handful of riders made it over to the lead group, but Dhaenens was not among them.

At the finish in the velodrome of Roubaix, he was 10 seconds behind as Eddy Planckaert beat Steve Bauer by less than an inch in a sprint. "It took some luck," Planckaert admitted. "To me, winning Paris–Roubaix is like winning the Tour de France. I'll never win the Tour because it's too hard and too mountainous. So this race has to mean the Tour de France to me."

Dhaenens will never win the Tour de France either and by now realizes that he will probably never win Paris–Roubaix. He recorded a fine ninth place among the 92 finishers and, as team leaders should, he was first across the line for PDM. "I was with a good group of riders but when I attacked, nobody would work with me," he said. "I took my chance and attacked and got near the leaders but nobody would work with me.

"Today I had good luck and might have won the race, but no. It'll never happen, I think."

Chapter 6
_____ Warming Up

There was no reason to worry, Greg LeMond kept saying, especially to himself, as he got off to a slow and painful start in the new season. His celebrity status in the United States — sportsman of the year for both *Sports Illustrated* magazine and ABC-TV's *Wide World of Sports*, television pitchman for Taco Bell fast foods — cost him weeks of vital training during the winter.

"One thing led to another and I found myself overwhelmed, too much to do," LeMond said of the commercial opportunities that followed his victory in the 1989 Tour de France. Having lived it up, LeMond was now painfully living it down.

"I'm hurting on hills," he admitted in March during the eight-day Paris–Nice race, in which he finished far down, more than eight minutes behind the winner, Miguel Indurain of the Banesto team. "I'm not bad, I'm just bad on the hills," LeMond said. He proved that a few hours later by finishing a minute behind the rest of his Z team during a long and hilly team time trial outside St. Étienne. Riding over 44.5 kilometers of wintry countryside, LeMond stayed with his teammates until the final long uphill ramp, where he was left behind.

"It was hard, a little too hard for me," he said as he pulled a jacket over the rainbow-striped jersey of the world champion. LeMond won that jersey a month after his second triumph in the Tour de France, which completed his comeback from a nearly fatal shooting accident in 1987. Remembering that long ordeal, he refused now to panic.

"No, no, no," he said hurriedly when asked if he was worried about his poor showings in races in Spain and France since early February. "Last year, if I was riding this way or if I got dropped on a hill, I'd worry and get thinking whether there was something wrong with me. Now I know nothing's wrong. It's just a matter of getting the kilometers in my legs.

I should be fine by May or June.

"Next year — each year I say 'next year' — I want to train well in January and be in good shape when the season starts. But it never happens."

Part of the problem was that when LeMond returned to Europe on Jan. 22 from the three-month layoff between seasons, he was far overweight. Some observers put the extra weight at 15 pounds but LeMond himself admitted to 4.4 kilograms (just under 9 pounds). He also reported that half that weight had since been lost.

"I'm at 74 kilos now," he said sheepishly, "still two kilos over my best weight. That's nearly five extra pounds to carry up each hill." He looked solid and explained that his extra weight was not fat but upper-body muscle developed while crosscountry skiing near his home in Wayzata, Minnesota. He trained hard during November and December, he said, mostly by rollerskiing and riding cyclocross, but a slight flu and business obligations had then cut short his roadwork.

"Everybody would like to see the world champion racing really well from February on, but my responsibility is to race really well in the Tour de France. As usual, that's my main goal."

Before the Tour in July, he expected to ride in some of the April classics, the Tour de Trump, the Giro d'Italia and the Tour of Switzerland. "I'm still hoping to win a classic, maybe Paris–Roubaix, but the two races I really want to do well in are the Tour de Trump and the Tour de France," he said. "The Tour de France for obvious reasons, the Tour de Trump because it's at home."

The pain and suffering that constitute the price of success were worth paying, he asserted. "I keep saying I'm suffering and it's hurting, but overall I can't complain. I'm extremely happy. I'm enjoying myself."

Two months later he could not say the same. By early May, the only consolation left for LeMond was gallows humor. Riding in the Tour de Trump before it reached its first serious climb outside Charlottesville, Virginia, LeMond found himself pedaling next to a car driven by an old friend, Mike Neel, formerly coach of the 7-Eleven team but now with Spago.

"How are you feeling?" Neel asked.

"Fine, just fine," LeMond answered. "I'm going to attack on the next descent." Attacks like that, with LeMond turning on the afterburners, had helped him win two Tours de France. But that was in another country and, besides, the legs are dead.

"Actually the only thing I'm good for is to attack from the finish line to the hotel," LeMond admitted. "I'm tired, real tired."

A few kilometers later he proved his point. As the road went uphill, he quickly fell behind and struggled in at the end of the stage 26 minutes behind the leaders. With the Tour de Trump not nearly half over, he was far out of contention. The world champion trailed amateur riders from New Zealand and West Germany, not to mention second-string professionals from Europe and the United States.

"I've started the year behind and I feel as if I'm always going to be behind," LeMond admitted in a despondent interview in Richmond. "I just haven't had any good period this year, not one race I felt good in at all. I'm really disappointed. I never expected my season to start this way."

As he well knew, the main problem was that it was not the start of the season. The professional year began in February and LeMond had not yet finished a race. Early in April he left his Z team in France to return to the United States. He was sick, he said, and needed to recover and train far from the pressure he feels in Europe. The month at his home in Minnesota, and at a training camp near Santa Rosa, California, did nothing to help him.

"I was completely dead till about a week and a half before this race," he said of the Tour de Trump, which began May 3 in Wilmington, Delaware, and ended 10 days later in Boston after covering 1,793 kilometers. "I was training, but nothing intense, some days just two or three hours. I literally was crawling on my bike for nearly four weeks."

His illness had not been diagnosed, he continued. He was tested for mononucleosis and hepatitis but proved negative.

All the doctors could report was that he had a virus.

"I just can't believe I'm not making much progress in my training," he said, still covered by the sweat and dirt of his ride. "Everybody else is at such a high level of condition. I feel pretty lousy right now and there's too much difference in ability out there."

In addition to his lost training and illness, he blamed his approaching 29th birthday. "I think that's a big part of it," he said. "My last memories of easy conditioning were in 1985–86, a good four or five years ago. I'm getting older and it's getting tougher to stay in top condition."

At the same time the year before, he was also experiencing difficulty, finishing 27th in the first Tour de Trump. But the problem then was medical, basically anemia. Diagnosed during the Giro d'Italia, the condition was cured with iron injections.

"I feel I'm in worse shape this year," LeMond said as he began to strip off his jersey. He was still a few pounds over his usual racing weight. The Tour de France was less than two months away and LeMond knew it. Another victory would remove all the disappointment of his year so far but, as he said, "I hate betting my season on winning the Tour de France."

His strategy was to ride himself back into shape. "If I can make it through this race and the Tour of Italy, I'm going to have a lot of good kilometers in me," he felt. "Either it's going to kill me and I'll never be good this year or else I'll be very good. It's going to be one or the other."

For the moment, he dared not guess which.

Tomorrow is Today

No more mañanas," said Raul Alcala. "No more eighth place, like last year. This time I hope to win the Tour de France. Why not? I feel pretty good, I have a lot of motivation. Sure, why not?"

Speaking by phone from his home in Switzerland, the

Mexican racer was offering the same upbeat assessment of chances that he gave in the United States after he won the Tour de Trump. Asked then if he thought he could win the Tour de France as well, he replied breezily, "Sure, why not?"

Now, a week before the Tour was to start in Futuroscope, the 'why nots' composed a long list, as Alcala admitted. They included Pedro Delgado, Laurent Fignon, Greg LeMond, Stephen Roche, Gianni Bugno, Charly Mottet, Andy Hampsten and Steven Rooks. To that list of favorites could be added such outsiders as Steve Bauer, Marino Lejarreta, Miguel Indurain, Fabio Parra, Sean Kelly and Erik Breukink.

"A lot of good riders, that's for sure," Alcala conceded. "But no one rider who's obviously the boss. LeMond should have been, but he's still not riding like last year. So it's a wide-open race. Why not me?"

Sure, why not? Then 26 years old, Alcala seemed finally to have developed into the mature and steady rider that the 7-Eleven team hoped for when it signed him out of Monterrey, Mexico, in 1986. With a fine ninth place in his second Tour de France in 1987 and the white jersey of the best young rider, followed by victory that year in the Coors Classic in Colorado, Alcala appeared to be headed for stardom.

It never happened, and his teammates blamed his preference for eating rather than training. In 1989 Alcala moved to the PDM team based in the Netherlands and enjoyed moderate success, winning a stage in the Tour. Always a strong climber, he had become an outstanding time trialer as well, winning the prologue in the Tour de Trump by a big seven seconds.

"This year is the first time I found a good position on a time trial bike," he explained. "Mostly it's that I'm in good shape and have the right amount of experience now."

As he knew, winning time trials was a key to winning. The 1990 Tour had five races against the clock, including the traditional short prologue and a team time trial. "My PDM team is riding very well, very strong," Alcala said. "They'll be a big help in that time trial."

In a major change from the previous Tour, the 1990 edition

was to end by reverting to the usual mass finish on the Champs-Élysées rather than a time trial like the one in which LeMond had made up a 50-second deficit to nip Fignon by 8 seconds for the final victory. As is often the case, the final time trial was now scheduled on the next-to-last day, at the Lac de Vassivière, where LeMond recorded the first Tour de France stage victory by an American, in 1985. By the last finish line, the field of 22 teams of nine riders each was to have covered 3,392.5 kilometers in a clockwise journey around France and a splinter of Switzerland.

Like many other observers, Alcala rated Delgado as the man to beat. The Spaniard won the Tour in 1988 and finished third the next year after a calamitous first two days in which he arrived 2 minutes 40 seconds late for the prologue — time that counted against him — and then collapsed in the team time trial. Before the race left its start in Luxembourg, Delgado was down 7 minutes and could regain only half of them by the finish in Paris.

Of the other favorites, at least two, Fignon and Roche, had medical problems. Roche, an Irishman, still had not demonstrated that he was fully recovered from a knee injury that forced him to quit the 1989 Tour halfway through. Fignon had crashed in the Giro d'Italia a month earlier, badly hurting his back and pelvis, which cost him 10 valuable days of training. Bugno, the easy winner of that Giro in his native country, was Alcala's choice of a dark horse. "If he keeps that form, we all better look out," the Mexican warned.

Could Bugno keep that form? Would Fignon and Roche overcome their injuries? Had LeMond recovered his best condition? Was Hampsten strong enough to last three weeks? Had Delgado bought himself a better watch? Was Alcala ready to bloom? Sure, why not?

"It is by riding a bicycle that you learn the contours of a country best, since you have to sweat up the hills and coast down them. Thus you remember them as they actually are, while in a motor car only a high hill impresses you."
— Ernest Hemingway.

Chapter 7

_____ The Prologue

With what almost sounded like a growl, Greg LeMond confirmed in Futuroscope what those closest to him had been saying. "I feel great, really strong," he reported. "I'm confident," and here his voice turned throaty, "very confident."

After an intense and painful series of races, the American insisted that he would be the man to beat when the Tour began. He was not alone in his optimism.

"Greg is very strong, healthy again," his wife, Kathy, said. Andy Bishop, a friend of LeMond's and a rider for 7-Eleven, agreed. "He has much better form than he had even a few weeks ago," Bishop reported. "He looks good, he looks healthy and his morale is really good."

Paul Koechli, the coach of the Helvetia team and LeMond's coach when he won the Tour de France for the first time in 1986, shared that view. "I saw in the Tour of Switzerland last week how he was regaining his form," Koechli said. "He's as good now as he's ever been, I think. For me, he's the main favorite."

Finally, Otto Jácome, LeMond's masseur and confidant, gave a fingertip analysis: "When I know he's aching, he's not going to win. Now he has no complaints, he's in good health and strong. He tells me, 'I feel power in my legs, I finish a stage and I feel strong.' From there, we take off."

LeMond seconded all these opinions. "I'm better at this time than I was a year ago at the start of the Tour," he said.

It had been another long way back. "I started from zero in

the Trump," he acknowledged. He struggled through that race, finishing 78th, then went to the three-week Giro d'Italia, where he reduced time lost in the mountains but again was no real factor, finishing 105th. He had only one good memory of the Giro: In one stage he had stopped to urinate at the side of the road and, just then, the pack took off. LeMond knows how to read the unwritten code of professional bicycle racing, which says that champions are not attacked while relieving themselves. In a rage, he mounted his bicycle and caught the pack, worked his way to the front and then attacked himself, going off on a 100-kilometer, two-man breakaway before he tired and was caught.

That was a flash of the old LeMond and better was to come the next week in the Tour of Switzerland. In that weeklong race he was able to stay with the leaders and finish the race in 10th place. He went home then to Marke, Belgium, and continued training, often behind a motorbike driven by Já-come. "I couldn't believe the speed I was hitting," LeMond said. "We'd get to 80 kilometers an hour and what I usually do is 60, maybe 70. Things are coming around.

"I've suffered a lot," he continued. "I didn't like being where I was, the world champion and Tour de France winner sick and struggling, but I knew there was nothing wrong with me. Last year was harder because I didn't know where I was. This year was harder for everybody else than it was for me.

"The Tour of Switzerland proved something to me. In the climbs in the Giro I lost 15 minutes each day in the mountains but in Switzerland I kept going, maybe losing a minute. I never really felt tired. I came out as fresh as when I started."

Despite his optimism, LeMond acknowledged that the Alps and Pyrenees would be a testing ground in the Tour. "You've just got to stay strong from start to finish in the Tour," he said. "You can try to gain a few seconds here and there but it always comes down to the mountains and the time trials. I'm looking forward to them.

"I'm feeling confident," he repeated, "really very confident."

Then he went out and showed exactly why.

As LeMond admits, after a decade of being a professional,

not too many races still motivate him. Of the few, the Tour de France ranks at the top of the list. In 1978, as a 17-year-old junior racer on his first trip to Europe, LeMond met a boyhood hero, Jean-Claude Killy, the winner of three gold medals in skiing at the 1968 Olympic Games in Grenoble, France, and they spent some hours cycling near the ski resort of Morzine. Just then the Tour de France went by.

"It was my first sight of professional racers," LeMond remembered years later. "I won't even pretend that I thought to myself, 'Someday I'll be riding in the Tour on that road,' but sure enough, in 1984 I did."

His first sight of the race enthralled LeMond. "I was awed by how many people were watching — a couple of hundred thousand spread along the course — and by how fit the riders were. They were like gods."

He was one of the gods himself now, a two-time winner of the Tour, a rider who had never finished a Tour off the final victory podium in Paris: third in 1984, second in 1985, first in 1986 and 1989. He hesitated to phrase it just this way but he felt he was a rider who couldn't lose the Tour unless he had medical problems, as in '84, or worked for his team leader, as in '85, or was simply not present, as in '87, after he was nearly killed in a hunting accident, and '88, when a tendon infection required surgery. When he rode healthy and for himself, LeMond believed, he had a mandate to win. He owed it to his talent.

Wearing *dossard* No. 1 and the yellow jersey of the previous Tour's winner, LeMond was last in the 198-man field to roll down the starting ramp and negotiate 6.3 kilometers through gusty winds sweeping across the arid plains of Futuroscope. He knew the time he had to beat: Thierry Marie of the Castorama team, a prologue specialist, had recorded 7 minutes 49 seconds, or four seconds better than the second-ranked rider, Raul Alcala.

For the prologue, LeMond was alone in using yet another technical innovation, a pair of triathlete bars that rose in a horn over his handlebars and included the gear shifter. The new straight-up bars, which he gripped hand over hand, kept him in a tight aerodynamic tuck. "I could get much more power," he said afterward of the bars that he developed with Boone Lennon. The pair had also developed the extended triathlete bars that LeMond used the year before to put away a Laurent Fignon doggedly riding toward the Champs-Élysées with standard handlebars. LeMond had a history of introducing accessories, like sunglasses and the handlebar-mounted bicycle computer, for both of which he was ridiculed in the years before nearly everybody in the pack began using them.

This time nobody laughed. The lesson of the final 1989 Tour time trial had sunk in. To reinforce it, LeMond clocked a splendid 7:53.14, or five-hundredths of a second faster than Alcala, for second place behind the untouchable Marie.

Prologues are just a way of adding a day to a race, satisfying the sponsoring municipality, and usually mean nothing. This one was different. The message was clear: LeMond was ready.

A Long Way Back

"So you made it back to the Tour de France?" an acquaintance asked Andy Bishop. "It wasn't easy."

"It sure wasn't," Bishop agreed. "First I had to drive to Lille, then fly to Nantes and then we drove to Poitiers. A long day."

For somebody with a degree from the University of Arizona in physics plus a minor in Russian, Bishop can sometimes be slow. Then he got the point of the question and broke into a wide smile. Making it back was more than a one-day journey. Earlier in the year, Bishop almost sank out of sight as a professional racer.

Instead of riding for the PDM team based in the Netherlands, rated first in the world in computerized standings, he rode in the spring of 1990 for the unheralded and low-budget American Commerce National Bank team. From his debut in the Tour in 1988 at age 23, he had dropped to the Phoenix Criterium and the La Jolla, California, Grand Prix.

It was a long way down and a long way back up, but Bishop

made it. When the 77th Tour de France began, he was wearing No. 84 as a member of the 7-Eleven team. Displaying nervousness, he finished the prologue in 128th place, 45 seconds behind Thierry Marie.

"I hope to prove something here," Bishop said before the start. "Not to PDM. I'm not vindictive. No, it's more to myself. If you prove something to yourself, that will prove it to everybody."

What he intended to prove was that he should not have finished the 1989 season without a single major professional team interested in signing him on. PDM declined to renew his two-year contract after sickness and lack of competition led to feeble showings in races.

"Part of it was my fault," Bishop admitted during the Tour de Trump, where he rode for the Spago team. "I realize now I didn't always work as hard as I should have, that I let my medical problems get the better of me."

He rode the Tour de Trump in hopes of attracting an employer for the European circuit, and fulfilled that goal with consistently strong daily results and a victory after a long breakaway on the stage into Harrisburg, Pennsylvania. Even before he finished a fine 13th in the Trump race, 7-Eleven had signed him to ride in the Giro d'Italia.

Back in Europe, Bishop flourished. And now he faced his second Tour de France, a race he remembered bittersweetly. He was considered too young and inexperienced to ride in the 1988 Tour but was rushed into action as a replacement for Greg LeMond, who could not start because of his infected right shin.

"I'm really excited because there's such an incredible difference between now and 1988," Bishop said. "Then I didn't know what to expect, and I was just dying the last week. I finished that Tour, and nobody can take that away, but it's no fun when you're just trying to survive." He ranked 132nd when the race ended.

"This is what cycling is all about," Bishop said, "and I have so much more fitness and strength than I did in '88. I can't wait."

Chapter 8
_____ Surprise Breakaway

Claudio Chiappucci realized how easy it would be to gain the jersey, white with red polka dots, of the Tour's best climber. There were just two climbs on the first stage, 138.5 kilometers from the high-tech tundra of Futuroscope out into prettily rolling countryside and then back to the theme park, and neither climb was demanding.

First was the Bonneuil hill, 18.5 kilometers from the start, with the Archigny hill 6 kilometers later. Both were rated fourth, and least, category in height, steepness and difficulty. Nevertheless they were worth points toward the climber's jersey and, over the years, some middling climbers had arrived in Paris in that jersey simply by scooping up points on hills and moderate mountains. Chiappucci, who won the climber's jersey in both Paris-Nice and the Giro d'Italia earlier in the year, knew that. He also knew that, because the Tour faced only one climb, again fourth category, on each of the next two days, the man in the climber's jersey wouldn't have much trouble defending it for a while.

So, at kilometer 6, off he jumped. Right behind the Italian rider with the Carrera team came Steve Bauer, a Canadian with 7-Eleven, Frans Maassen, a Dutchman with Buckler, and Ronan Pensec, a Frenchman with Z. "I knew that the morning stage before the team time trial is a good one to attack on," Bauer said later. "Nobody really wants to chase and wear himself out before the time trial."

For the next 24 kilometers, their lead ranged from 20 to 30 seconds. As he hoped, Chiappucci was first over the two hills, disappointing Bauer, who had also hoped to spend a few days in the climber's jersey. Maassen's ambition was similar: He wanted to win the first bonus sprint, at kilometer 34, and gain the green points jersey. Pensec was along only to show his face, he confessed. The year before had been a washout for him and the Z team's sponsor had publicly shown his loss of confidence in Pensec by replacing him as leader with Greg LeMond. "I just wanted to let everybody see that I was still around," Pensec explained.

It was, in other words, a standard breakaway, with each rider having his own small reasons for attacking and nobody thinking big thoughts. "All four of us were just rolling along, nothing fast until we turned it up a bit for the bonus sprint," Bauer remembered. "Suddenly we were two minutes ahead." Behind them the pack had given up the chase, and that was a mistake.

By kilometer 40, the lead was up to 2 minutes 50 seconds and by kilometer 55 it was 5 minutes. At kilometer 87, the leaders sped through the town of Lussac les Chateaux more than 11 minutes ahead. The lead reached its apex of 13 minutes about 10 kilometers from the finish, as the glass towers of Futuroscope glinted on the horizon.

The pack woke up then and was able to reduce the lead to 10:35 as Maassen went over the line first, followed by Pensec, Chiappucci and Bauer. When the two bonus sprints and the time bonus for winning were factored in, Bauer was in the yellow jersey by two seconds over Maassen because of the Canadian's better time in the prologue — 21 seconds behind Thierry Marie, for 19th place, against the Dutchman's loss of 35 seconds, for 73d place.

For somebody who just wanted to remind the pack that he was still around, Pensec was both jubilant and baffled. "I can't explain it," he said. "How can you figure that they allowed us to get that far ahead?"

He was not alone in asking the question. The obvious answer was given by Gerard Rué of Castorama, who said, "The team that rolls in the morning is sure to pay in the afternoon." Laurent Fignon, Rué's teammate, shared that view. "It was a trap," he said. "One hundred forty kilometers in the morning before the team time trial was too long. Over that distance, the team that leads the pursuit is going to have to really work. And in the afternoon it will pay. So nobody wanted to ride."

Pedro Delgado had an explanation of his own. After an

early flat, he had to work hard with his teammates to rejoin the pack and then, with about 60 kilometers left, the Spaniard crashed, bruising his backside and right shoulder.

Why had he crashed?

The Tour was trying hard to keep it quiet, but there had been a demonstration by sheep farmers who were protesting a cut in government subsidies and increased lamb imports from other countries of the Common Market and Eastern Europe. Their real income, the shepherds explained, as they stopped reporters' cars by blocking the road with branches and bales of wool, had declined 15 percent in the last three years. The motorcycle police who travel with the Tour got to the blockade pretty quickly and cleared a path, but somebody poured oil on the road and Delgado was one of a dozen riders who lost control of their bicycles and fell. Bruised and angry, he was in no mood to chase down the attack.

Greg LeMond understood both sides of the problem. "If I was on another team, I would have panicked," he said. "But since it was Ronan up front, it was up to the others to work. I understand Fignon's attitude: The team that leads the chase is sacrificing itself for the others."

Predictably, some of the old-timers traveling with the Tour were outraged about the four-man breakaway. In their day, they let it be known, this would not have been allowed. In their day, riders worked for a leader and only for that leader, not for themselves. In their distant and now irrelevant day, there were still rules.

Thus Luis Ocaña, winner of the 1973 Tour, recalled the start of that race. "José Catieau, my teammate, went off with Herman van Springel in the first stage, trying to take the yellow jersey. That night, at our hotel, I took my shower and went downstairs with my suitcase packed. I said to Maurice De Muer, our coach: 'You choose. Him or me.' A subordinate, you see, doesn't have the right to do his own number. If I had been LeMond, when the breakaway reached two minutes, I would have made my team roll and wiped it out, no matter if Pensec was ahead."

(The old timers knew how to deal with the ambitious

domestique, Geoffrey Nicholson relates in his classic book, "The Great Bike Race." When Johan de Muynck began attacking his Brooklyn team leader, Roger de Vlaeminck, in the 1976 Giro, he found himself isolated even though he was in second place overall, trailing Felice Gimondi by just 19 seconds. In the deciding time trial, Brooklyn refused to have a team car follow de Muynck, who had to rely on a Belgian television commentator to carry his spare wheels. He did not make up the 19 seconds and Brooklyn did not mourn the loss.)

Bernard Hinault, who rode a decade after Ocaña, when teams were beginning to turn away from domination by a single leader, was more reasonable. "I never would have allowed the attack to develop such a lead," he wrote in his daily column in *l'Équipe*. "The most they should have been allowed was five minutes." If Ocaña swore that the favorites had dug themselves a deep grave, Hinault went no further than to say they had committed a tactical error.

Delgado was coming around to that point of view. "Maybe we've made a mistake," he said. "Bauer isn't going to be easy to bring back."

Fignon disagreed. "Ten minutes, that's a lot, but it's not everything. This year Bauer isn't climbing well. Pensec can lose seven minutes in the first time trial and Chiappucci showed his limitations in the Giro. You can't think of them as dangerous riders."

Not everybody was so sure. For Cyrille Guimard, Fignon's coach, the real threat was neither Bauer nor Pensec but Chiappucci. That seemed strange, since Bauer had finished as high as fourth in the Tour in 1988 and had worn the yellow jersey and grown accustomed to its pressure. Pensec, too, had placed high in the Tour — sixth in 1986, seventh in 1988. But Chiappucci? At age 27 and in his sixth season with Carrera, he had a total of four victories, including a stage in Paris–Nice and in the Tour of Sicily. In 1989 he had finished a mere 81st in the Tour. He was not even the team leader with Carrera, a role reserved for Flavio Giupponi after he finished second to Fignon in the '89 Giro. Giupponi had done nothing since that race and Chiappucci had been given the right to ride for himself.

Perhaps Guimard had been impressed by his climbing ability in the Giro. Whatever the reason, if Guimard saw something, people went back for a second look. Since he retired from a moderately successful career as a racer and became a *directeur sportif* in 1976, Guimard had guided three men to seven victories in the Tour. They were Lucien Van Impe in 1976, Hinault in 1978, '79, '81 and '82 and Fignon in 1983 and '84. His riders had won the Vuelta de España twice and the Giro three times. LeMond, who often feuded with him, still said that Guimard was the one former *directeur sportif* of his he most respected for his sense of strategy.

How important is strategy? Not too important to such fans as France's President François Mitterrand, who once explained professional bicycle racing to a visiting American academic by saying, "Strategy is arriving before anyone else."

For the moment, that defined the four breakaways.

Serious About His Work

This was as meaningless as a race could be: Platoons of riders leaving in six heats, with the times of the winners ranked to determine the overall winner of the inconsequential preface to a Tirreno–Adriatico stage race in Italy. Almost nobody cared how he did — except Steve Bauer, who went all out and bettered the previous leading time by more than a minute.

"You took it pretty seriously," an acquaintance told Bauer.

"It was a bike race," said Bauer, a stern look crossing his face. "You have to take it seriously."

The Canadian had been taking racing seriously since he decided that he was not big enough or fast enough to become a professional hockey player. The results had been impressive, including his wearing the yellow jersey for five days in the 1988 Tour before finally finishing fourth.

After that high point, the season ended in catastrophe as Bauer collided with Claude Criquelion as they both led the charge over the final 50 meters in the world championship road race in Belgium that year. Bauer, who recovered to finish second to Maurizio Fondriest, was disqualified 'for actions deliberately unsportsmanlike and dangerous' in seeming to have elbowed Criquelion, causing him to fall as the Belgian was trying to pass on the inside along the crowd barriers. After the crash, Criquelion walked across the line, dragging his battered bicycle, and finished 11th.

Once before Bauer had come close to a major victory. In the 1984 Olympic road race in Los Angeles, he took the lead near the finish by passing Alexi Grewal of the United States, who was staggering. "When I caught him, I was tired," Bauer remembered years later, "but I'd done a one-kilometer, flat-out sprint, and when I got him, I went by quickly. But if you look at the videotape, I kept going hard for an extra 500 meters and he responded very quickly and was right on my wheel. It was like lightning hit him. Everyone thought he was dead, but he wasn't — not completely." They rode on together, comfortably ahead of the pack, and in the final sprint Grewal just managed to get across the line first.

"It was rare that Alexi and I would come to a head-to-head sprint, but normally, maybe eight times out of ten, I'd beat him," Bauer continued. "Obviously he recuperated on my wheel and he had that extra snap. That was all there was to it."

The silver medal meant a lot to him and to Canada, he said. "It gave my popularity a big boost and cycling's popularity too. Before, people didn't really know what cycling was all about."

He was proof of that, he conceded, when he was growing up in Fenwick, Ontario, 90 miles west of Toronto. When his parents, both schoolteachers, gave him his first bicycle, an Eddy Merckx model, Bauer could not quite place the name. "I sort of knew Merckx had won the world championship road race in Montreal, but not much more than that."

A month after the 1984 Olympics, Bauer turned professional with La Vie Claire and went to the world championships in Barcelona, where he placed third in the road race to

Criquelion. "Coming third was just a reinforcement that I would be a worthwhile international rider," Bauer said. "It gave me a lot of confidence that I knew I could win a big race.

"I didn't think that professional racing would be easy. You have to be realistic. No matter what race it is, it's never easy. The funny thing is that when you do win and look back on it, you think, 'It wasn't so hard after all.' But to get there is never easy."

Holding on to the Yellow Jersey

More than a few people expected Steve Bauer to lose the yellow jersey in the afternoon stage, the team time trial. Down only two seconds, Frans Maassen had the Buckler power-house to tow him along in a discipline long favored by Dutch teams. His own *directeur sportif*, Jan Raas, had been a locomotive of the Raleigh team, now Panasonic, in the team race against the clock.

Nevertheless Bauer was optimistic. "We expect to do really well in the time trial," he said as the 7-Eleven team waited in a huge parking lot to be called to the start line. "We're looking for a finish in the top three."

That would have been astounding, as Bauer understood, but a team leader, especially when he is ahead in the Tour de France, is supposed to be optimistic. Once the 44.5-kilometer race began on a blustery and overcast day, Bauer had a hard time backing up his words. Showing the effects of the long breakaway, he was slow to contribute as each rider took a short pull at the front to set a continually high pace. A third of the way into the stage, Bauer grew stronger and 7-Eleven began moving.

At the 20-kilometer checkpoint, the team was six seconds behind Buckler's time. From then on, the gap began changing and 7-Eleven finally came in at 54 minutes 12 seconds, or 8 seconds better than Buckler. Bauer's prediction was off by three places as the team finished sixth, good enough to keep him in the yellow jersey.

Immediately behind 7-Eleven, in seventh place, was Z, and its riders wanted only to talk about how strongly Greg LeMond had ridden. "We were going like a 10-man team, not a 9-man one," Eric Boyer said. "LeMond did the work of two riders." LeMond was continuing to send messages to the pack.

A Return to Their Roots

In some quarters the early breakaway on the stage before the team time trial is known as the Alex Stieda Gambit, so called for the Canadian rider with 7-Eleven who won the yellow jersey that way in 1986 and became the first North American ever to lead the Tour.

Early in the stage, through the suburban sprawl west of Paris, Stieda, then 25 years old, jumped away. Before he was caught, he had won enough bonus sprints and minor climbs to wind up with four jerseys in addition to the yellow one: white for best young rider, red for leader in bonus sprints, polka dot for best climber, and patchwork for best all-around rider.

"Just super, wonderful, unbelievable," he said after his 85-kilometer jaunt. "I went as hard as I could as long as I could." He was caught 10 kilometers from the finish but hung on to take fifth place.

His glory was short-lived. In the afternoon stage, a 48-kilometer team time trial, 7-Eleven finished next to last in the 21-team field because it had to wait for Stieda, who barely managed to avoid elimination as he struggled along. "He was shot, wasted," explained a teammate, Davis Phinney. "We were fighting a strong headwind and after 20 kilometers he had nothing left after his ride this morning."

Stieda finished three minutes behind his team. From yellow jersey in the morning, he finished the day in 116th place overall. Worse, his performance helped humiliate 7-Eleven, which was clocked six minutes behind the winner and ahead of only the maladroit Café de Colombia team.

Times had changed. From an American-Canadian-Mexican team in its first Tour, 7-Eleven had bulked up with such good Europeans as Dag-Otto Lauritzen of Norway and Sean Yates of Britain in addition to Bauer. A training camp to polish its skills in the team time trial shortly before the Tour showed how professional the American team now was.

Behind this, though, the truth was that 7-Eleven had reached a plateau and not an overly high one. This became evident in the Tour de Trump earlier in the year, when Andy Hampsten, in ninth place, was the only 7-Eleven rider in the top 20 and the team itself finished sixth, behind such overachievers as AC Pinarello, Spago and Subaru-Montgomery. Other than the team time trial, no stage was won by 7-Eleven, which could boast of just a handful of almosts.

"We came in as heavy favorites and a lot of pressure was put on our shoulders, and sometimes we made a few tactical mistakes — maybe we chased a little bit too hard or we waited too long," said the thoughtful Ron Kiefel. "This is bicycle racing," he continued. "Sometimes you have the luck, sometimes everything falls your way, and sometimes you have little problems here and there and they add up."

The riders all denied they were disappointed, which is a sign of either hard-headed professionalism (some races you win, some you lose, but your confidence is unshaken) or weary indifference (nothing had gone quite right in a year, and one more botched opportunity meant little).

As usual, the truth was somewhere in between. What seemed obvious was that 7-Eleven lacked the attacking mindset that brought it victories in its earliest European appearances, starting with a stage victory in the Giro in 1985 a week after the riders turned professional. Over the years, two victories in the Tour of Switzerland, one in the Giro and four stage victories in the Tour de France added to the luster.

The current lack of offense first became noticeable in the 1989 Tour, where the team was overly reactive rather than creative and daring. Gone were the hit-and-run tactics of early days; replacing them was a stodgy, establishment wait-and-see strategy.

The Tour de Trump was crucial to 7-Eleven, which faced an uncertain future because its sponsor, the Southland Corp., was sinking in a sea of junk-bond debt. If it hoped to attract another corporate bankroller, the team needed good publicity.

Speaking after the Trump race about forthcoming appearances in such major European races as the Giro and the Dauphiné Libéré, Phinney admitted, "We have to win there or we're in trouble." Many observers would even have said big trouble. In fact, neither the Giro nor the Dauphiné went well for 7-Eleven. Basking now in its fine showing in the Tour time trial and with its leader in yellow, the team appeared to be on the rebound.

Chapter 9
_____ Italian Renaissance

Some people want to do good, but Moreno Argentin wants simply to do well. And he often has: In the decade since the Italian rider turned professional, he won the world championship road race in 1986 and finished second the next year, won his country's national championship in 1983 and 1989, won the Tour of Lombardy in 1987, the Tour of Flanders in 1990 and Liège–Bastogne–Liège in 1985, '86 and '87.

Otherwise Argentin has bad luck.

Let Greg LeMond tell about the world championship of 1984 in Barcelona: "He admitted later that he had something against me from the '83 worlds, when I won," LeMond said. "I had dropped him and he'd been taking a lot of bad press at home in Italy because he hadn't been able to stay with me, so the next year in Barcelona he sat right on my wheel the whole race," drafting. "I mean that: all race long! Any move I made, he was right there on my wheel, never helping out by letting me draft off his wheel to save some energy. I ended up watching 20 guys jump away with no effort at all, just riding away from me because they were working together, and I had nobody except Argentin, sitting behind me. 'What's wrong?' I asked him. 'Why are you doing this? What have you got against me?'

"He said something like, 'We're friends, but give me some money, $10,000, and I'll work for you.' To be truthful, I knew at the time it was sarcasm, said only to get me even angrier. But I was so angry that I decided not to take it. When the race ended, I told the press, 'He wanted money, he told me so.' I wish now I'd never done it because the controversy hurt Argentin tremendously, but it also taught him not to fool around with me. He gave away the world championship. He could have won that year as easily as I could have if we'd worked together. It was very upsetting to me the way he acted and I certainly upset him when I told about his demanding money, but at the time I felt he deserved it. Italian journalists asked, 'Greg, why didn't you win?' I said, 'Argentin sat on my wheel and then wanted $10,000 to race.' Boy, did that raise a storm in Italy for him."

That was just one bit of bad luck. A few years later Argentin provoked the *tifosi*, the superheated horde of Italian cycling fans, by moving to Monte Carlo to escape taxes at home. A couple of years after that, in a Tirreno–Adriatico race, he swung at a traffic officer who he felt was blocking his way and found himself accused of physically assaulting a policeman in the pursuit of his duties. As crimes go, it was surely not the most outrageous committed in Naples that day, but it was enough to make the headlines and stigmatize a rider who had never won many hearts.

Now Argentin was popular again. The retirement of one major Italian bicycling star, Francesco Moser, and the decline of another, Giuseppe Saronni, had something to do with it. Another factor was Argentin's new work ethic. Victory in the Tour of Flanders and fourth place in Milan–San Remo had lofted him atop the World Cup standings when the Tour began. A stage victory in the Tour of Switzerland a few weeks before had consolidated his position. Like so many of the Italian riders, whose world is circumscribed by the Giro, he had never entered the Tour de France before. But then his sponsor, Ariostea, a manufacturer of kitchen ceramics, decided in 1990 that publicity would help in the coming monetary union of Europe.

Argentin admitted that he was not a candidate for the final yellow jersey. "I'm a realist," he said. "I know I'm a rider for the classics, not stage races." This third stage especially seemed right for him: 228 rolling kilometers from Poitiers to Nantes, the only climbing difficulty a fourth-category hill two-thirds of the way along.

On this rainy day, however, the trick was to reach the bitty hill, the Mont des Alouettes. The Tour was once again the target of protesters. Not the sheep farmers of the Vienne, who had made their peace at the start by awarding a lamb to a baffled Fabio Parra of the Kelme team. The explanation was that Kelme had finished last in the team time trial, like (ready for it?) a lamb led to slaughter. Still chuckling, the shepherds tucked their hefty staves under their arms and trudged off to their meadows.

From different meadows, those of the regions of Deux Sèvres and the Vendée, where more pugnacious shepherds frolic, came the next band of demonstrators. Not for them the throwing of branches across the road and the spilling of oil to interrupt the race. These two dozen farmers didn't plan merely to interrupt, but to end. Near the town of St. Gemme, 86 kilometers into the stage, four trees blocked the road while burning bales of hay and piles of tires marked the barricades with dark smoke amid a heavy drizzle. Banners announced that the race was to be stopped to protest agricultural quotas and lamb imports.

A way around the demonstration had to be found and it was, guided at one point by a local youth on a bicycle as the Tour de France took to the backroads for 20 kilometers to skirt the protesters. With the pack grouped, the race was easily neutralized. The riders glided along with the same insouciance they show daily between the ceremonial start and the real start, those few kilometers, that comfort zone, where no attack is permitted and every man is allowed to dream lightly of triumph ahead.

If the riders were no more than sulky, Bernard Hinault was angry. Everybody remembered how he had punched out at shipyard workers when they blocked the road in the 1984 Paris–Nice race. He raised sheep himself, Hinault said, or had somebody do it for him, and so he was basically sympathetic to the demonstrators' anger. That did not diminish his outrage. "Five or six thousand people have lost their chance to see the Tour go by," he said. "Cycling is always exposed to this type of demonstration. Why? Simply because it's free. It's not like tennis or soccer, which never has this type of problem because a seat is too expensive to waste it in a protest."

Other officials tried harder to conceal their chagrin. "The Tour de France is vulnerable because it uses public roads and because it offers such good publicity to a disruption," said Jean-Marie Leblanc, the director of the race. He also noted the obvious, that one group of workers had interfered with another's right to work. It had been a stormy day, Leblanc said, figuratively and literally.

Intermittent heavy rain had left the roads slick, causing a series of crashes. Laurent Fignon was one of those who went down hard. "Two Spaniards fell right in front of me and I couldn't avoid them," he reported. One of the Spaniards, Roque de la Cruz, of the Seur team, became the first rider to drop out of the Tour when he had to be taken to a hospital for his injuries. Fignon had also been slowed by a puncture in the early going and had to ride all-out to make it back to the pack, where he finished in 169th place without losing time on the overall leaders.

In Fignon, the Castorama team had a man nearly at the tail of the pack and, in Christophe Lavainne, another nearly at the front. After a packed sprint finish, Lavainne hurled his arms aloft in victory as he outlasted Uwe Raab of PDM and Olaf Ludwig of Panasonic. What Lavainne didn't know was that Argentin had crossed the same line alone 2 minutes 29 seconds earlier.

It happens now and again. Why had Lavainne celebrated? "Because I didn't know Argentin was ahead." How could he not know? "There are 200 riders, you can't know what everybody is doing. Nobody told me Argentin was up ahead of us."

With 50 kilometers to go, the Italian went for it. He chose his spot carefully, about 15 kilometers before a feed zone, which he stormed through without wasting time to grab a *musette*, or meal bag. Soon his lead was 1:20, and rose consistently while the rest of the pack slowed to grab and pack away their *musettes* of small sandwiches, pastries and fruits. With 20 kilometers left, Argentin was 4 minutes ahead when he failed to handle a sloshy curve and crashed. Another piece of bad luck, but he was back on his bicycle quickly and strong enough to keep most of his lead.

While many of the sprinters were preparing to kick into overdrive, Argentin was having his wounds bandaged and preparing to accept the ritual victory bouquet wrapped in cellophane.

A pretty tough day? Lavainne was asked. "Let's see," he replied. "There was Fignon's crash, the rain and the demonstration. I think that makes a tough day for anybody."

Not Dead, Only Sleeping

In a celebrated obituary in 1989, *La Gazzetta dello Sport* pronounced Italian cycling dead. All the vital signs were missing, said the Italian paper, pointing to the few and unimportant races that its country's professional riders had won in recent years. Finding no trace of breath, *La Gazzetta* removed the mirror from the corpse's lips, shrugged and walked away in sorrow.

La Gazzetta is to Italian cycling what Brooks Brothers is to seersucker suits: a defender of the faith. But this time it got it wrong. Early in the 1990 season, as in a scary movie, the body began stirring, the eyelids began flickering and color returned to the cheeks. What was this talk of rigor mortis when Gianni Bugno opened the World Cup season with a victory in Milan–San Remo? When Claudio Chiappucci won the mountain climbing jersey in Paris–Nice? When Moreno Argentin won the Tour of Flanders? When Argentin jumped to the top of the World Cup standings? When Marco Giovannetti won the Vuelta de España, the world's third-ranked stage racre?

Certo, the days of Francesco Moser and Giuseppe Saronni are over. Roberto Visentini rides now for a minor team and rarely, if ever, crosses the border to compete. The sensitive Maurizio Fondriest appeared unable to regain the form and luck that made him world champion in 1988. Flavio Giupponi was evidently a flash in the pan and his second place to Laurent Fignon in the 1989 Giro d'Italia may be the high point of his career.

But the Italian Renaissance was in full sway, as the 1990 Giro proved. Bugno won the prologue and held the pink jersey for the rest of the race, becoming the second rider in modern times, after Eddy Merckx, to have led the Giro from wire to wire. He excelled in the mountains and in the time trials. For the first time in years, the *tifosi* heard their hearts sing.

The music was, of course, by Mozart. Somewhere between the composer's Haffner symphony (Köchel 385) and his Jupiter (K. 551), Bugno learned, *allegro vivace*, how to become a champion. Given a month of musical therapy to cure vertigo, Bugno blossomed from a timid rider who seemed able to win only small races into the man who led the computerized rankings of the world's top 600 professionals.

One of his undetected problems was vertigo, or dizziness and fear of falling when he descended from a mountain peak at high speed. Bugno finally bared the secret after he was first over the top in the 1989 Milan–Turin classic but was easily caught by the pack on the descent. "A priest in a soutane could have made it down faster than I did," Bugno admitted. "I felt so dizzy that I slowed down almost to a stop."

The trouble was laid to a bad crash in the 1988 Giro and to a congenital obstruction in the canals of his inner ear. As a cure, Bugno tried ultrasound treatments laced with music. "I listened to Mozart at different speeds and degrees of loudness for a month," he said. "After that, the vertigo was gone."

Then he visited an allergist, who discovered that he could not tolerate wheat, milk and milk products. A combination of pills was prescribed and his diet was changed.

Afterward he was put into the hands of Claudio Corti, a veteran Italian rider, who taught Bugno how to take charge of his Chateau d'Ax team.

Finally he began seeing a psychologist, who helped resolve Bugno's timidity. This problem was traced to his childhood, which he spent with his grandparents in Italy while his parents worked in Switzerland. (Bugno was born in Brigg, Switzerland, where his father was a carpenter.)

All this took place in the 1989–90 off-season. The rider who had won only the minor Tour of Calabria in 1988, the Tour of the Appenines in 1986, '87 and '88 and the semi-classic Tour of Piedmont in 1986 suddenly was storming down the Poggio hill to win Milan–San Remo while other riders took the descent more prudently and slowly.

His victory in the Giro was just as impressive, with Bugno finishing first by 6 minutes 33 seconds. Even so, many Italians advised him to skip the Tour de France, reasoning that he had nothing further to prove and that his chances were slim. No Italian has won the Tour since 1965.

"The Italians just aren't used to such a hard race," judged Bernard Thévenet, who won the Tour de France twice in the 1970s. "And, coming a month after the Giro, the Tour is just too much for most riders who went all-out in Italy."

Bugno knew that. He had finished 68th in 1988 and 11th the next year. But, as he said, "The Tour de France is the summit of cycling: more fans than any other race, more reporters, more pressure. I still have a lot to learn, but if I didn't feel I had a role to play, I wouldn't be here."

"I think I'm going to get some new respect," he added, and he might have been speaking for all Italian riders. Hold the embalming fluid, *La Gazzetta dello Sport*.

Chapter 10

_____ Regionals' Day

Even such a vast and imposing event as the Tour de France still has occasional room in its heart for the personal touch. Better: the personal touch with tradition behind it.

About 70 kilometers from the finish of the fourth stage, just outside the town of Bedée in Brittany, the pack allowed Gerard Rué to go off ahead, alone. Ordinarily Rué, a teammate of Laurent Fignon's with Castorama and the winner of the Midi Libre stage race just the month before, would have rated a counterattacker or two, domestiques from the other French teams who would ride his wheel and make sure that he was not slipping off to try to steal a victory. This time, though, the pace remained moderate.

The explanation was that Rué was 'the regional,' as the local hero is called. He came from Bedée and his parents still lived there. They would be waiting with assorted cousins, uncles and aunts up the road to welcome Rué back home. The tradition of the *bon de sortie*, or permission for a rider to leave, is many decades old in the Tour, and touching. In its small way, it manages to say that the riders are not heroes isolated from their roots, but still part of the fabric of small-town France.

The Tour works hard to keep its reputation as a *fete populaire*, or people's party: Each morning, in the half hour or so between the beginning of the ritual sign-in and the start, riders and their public meet. Old men turn up in racing jerseys of teams long extinct to glide on their bicycles among the riders and mimic — but never, even to the coldest eye, parody — the sport of youth. The police are lenient about letting children pass through the barriers and seek autographs. The time passes quickly with a word with a rider here, a 'good luck' whispered to an idol there. It means nothing and is never forgotten.

So Rué played out his part in the ceremony, shaking

hands, exchanging kisses on first this cheek, then that, then again on each for the maximum of four kisses that the French reserve for family and closest friends. A few banalities were exchanged too: "All goes well, Gerard?" his mother asked. He assured her that it did. "All goes well?" his father asked, and was reassured in turn.

All began to go less well as the pack neared and Gilles Delion popped off the front and sped away. A Frenchman with the Helvetia team based in Switzerland, Delion was emphatically not a regional, since he was born hundreds of miles from Brittany in St. Étienne and has lived most of his life even further east, in Chambéry in the Alps. In short, he had not been granted a *bon de sortie* — he was attacking, and now the pack was forced to react. He is young, ambitious and coltishly rapid, not the sort of rider to be allowed much leeway. (Delion apologized later for his breach of pack etiquette, explaining that he had not known a regional was up ahead, visiting his family.) With a smile, Rué got back on his bicycle, waited for the pack and then pedaled off to join the chase.

The last 60 kilometers of the 203-kilometer stage were raced at high speed, with one attacker after another allowed his head for a while and then caught. First it was the solitary Delion, then Edwig van Hooydonck of the Buckler team with him, before Panasonic pulled the pack along to chase them both down. Off went Soren Lilholt of the Histor team and built a lead approaching one minute during his 38-kilometer breakaway before William Pulido of Postobon and Kurt Steinmann of Weinmann went after him. Lilholt, a Dane, is a specialist at this sort of doomed breakaway, going off once or twice each Tour de France, while knowing in his heart that he cannot steal a stage: He is just strong enough to stay ahead over a long distance but not quite strong enough to open a lead that will last as his pursuers ride him down. The laws of motion dictate that, other factors being equal, a field of riders taking short turns in setting the pace will always go faster than a man alone, and so it was once again for Lilholt. Fifteen kilometers from the finish everybody was together and riding fast.

Four kilometers further along, disaster! Suddenly the road narrowed because large bales of hay had been placed to block riders from taking a wrong turn — or a shortcut — at a traffic circle. Possibly the bales had been pushed even more into the road by the spectators behind them. Riders who had been three and four abreast, bumping shoulders while keeping their bicycles inches apart, had to funnel into a stretch where not more than two and perhaps only one might pass. The leaders got through in a steady flow, but behind them the pace had to slacken and the long line of the pack grew longer still. There were some crashes, with riders down on the ground. Others managed to keep their balance although they had to stop and wait for those ahead to move through the bottleneck.

"If you want to avoid crashes, the place to be is up front," Greg LeMond said later, restating an old truth. Then again, LeMond was up front. Less lucky were some of the other favorites, such as Laurent Fignon, Gianni Bugno and Pedro Delgado.

"I committed the error of letting myself drift to the tail end of the pack," Bugno admitted. "I wasn't vigilant, that's all." He had enough luck to find a few teammates near him and they began laboriously working their way back toward the front, moving from one small group of riders to the next group ahead. Delgado latched on and, three kilometers from the finish, they finally were within sight of the leaders.

By that time they were all being buffetted by strong sea winds along the causeway to Mont St. Michel, an island except for those two times a day when the tide was farthest out in the bay leading to the English Channel.

Do riders have much opportunity to look at the scenery? Sometimes yes, especially in the first few slow hours of a flat stage. This is the social period, a chance to chat with a friend from another team, to pass along a joke or piece of gossip heard at the previous night's hotel, to notice the change of crops in the outlying fields if the race has moved into a new region. France is such a small country really, the size of

Texas, and so specific in its farming that days can pass with nothing but long fields of sunflowers, grown for their oil, lining the road. Then the riders enter sheep-raising country with not a sunflower to be seen on the green and rolling meadows.

On this stage, however, the racing was so difficult that nobody was able to look up at the approaching Mont St. Michel, until the eighth century Mont Tombe, one of the mythological tombs at sea where souls were ferried after death. For a millennium Mont St. Michel and its raging tides had been visited by pilgrims, tourists and warriors, but never before by the Tour de France. This visit was part of a campaign by a new, young mayor representing the island's 150 voters. "We want to show that the Mont is first a living community, that it's not simply the eighth wonder of the world," explained Eric Vannier, the mayor and coincidentally owner of Mont St. Michel's main restaurant. He had plans, too, for an arts festival, fireworks and a bigger and better sound and light show. Vannier shrugged off complaints about the tackiness of the main street and its shops and stalls with trashy souvenirs. "It's what the tourists want," he told *l'Équipe.*

All is not commercialism on the Mont, the paper found, interviewing the resident three monks and two nuns of the Order of St. Benoit. At the Sunday mass two days before the Tour de France arrived, Father André spoke about the race in his homily, pointing out the human, Christian and positive values of the race. He cited particularly its sense of teamwork and effort.

Straining over their handlebars, trying to fight the gusty winds, the riders would have agreed. On the causeway, Olaf Ludwig of Panasonic, a fine East German sprinter, spotted the big red Coca-Cola van that is usually parked at the finish to supply well-televised drinks to the riders. Ludwig jumped for what he mistook for the finish, taking with him such other sprinters as Eric Vanderaerden of Buckler, Uwe Raab of PDM and Davis Phinney of 7-Eleven. "We cursed when we realized the finish was still 500 meters away," Phinney said. Jelle

Nijdam of Buckler then made his move but was passed by Johan Museeuw of Lotto, who held off Guido Bontempi of Carrera and a resurgent Ludwig and Phinney.

Last in the first pack of 50 riders to finish in the same time as Museeuw was Steve Bauer, who kept the yellow jersey and gained time on his closest rivals. LeMond was 40th in the group of 50, gaining seven seconds on Raul Alcala and Stephen Roche, who were unable to bridge when the pack split just in front of them along the causeway. Bigger losers were Bugno and Delgado, 21 seconds back in the third group, and the biggest of all the favorites was Fignon, 44 seconds behind in 140th place for the stage. The man who had lost the Tour de France by 8 seconds the year before knew far too well how important 44 seconds could be.

Bad Boy of the Sport

The Nantes–Mont St. Michel stage was crowded with 'regionals.' In addition to the Breton Gerard Rué, there were four Normans: Jean-Claude Bagot of St. Hilaire du Harcouet and the RMO team; François Lemarchand of Livarot and the Z team, and two riders for Castorama, Thierry Marie of Bénouville and Vincent Barteau of Caen.

L'Équipe had the smart idea of asking each what Mont St. Michel meant to him. Bagot said: "For a Norman, it's a fantastic site. If it's good weather, you have an unforgettable vista. The boys who haven't seen it are going to be thrilled." Lemarchand said: "I've only been there once, but there's nothing more beautiful. It's truly a marvel. It's marvelous." Marie said: "For me, it's something anchored, like the Tour de France. When I was a kid, I used to go with my father to admire Bernard Hinault in the Tour de France and Mont St. Michel. I dream about winning the stage." Barteau said: "Nothing special to me. Absolutely nothing. It's beautiful, I agree, but who cares?"

Vintage Vince. Among other wonders that he once thought were nothing special was the yellow jersey of the Tour de

France. Barteau spent two weeks in the yellow jersey in the 1984 Tour after a long three-man breakaway gave him a lead of more than 17 minutes over most of the pack. He was disconsolate then, having finished second on the stage to an obscure Portuguese rider, Paulo Ferreira. "Of course I'm disappointed," Barteau said as he slipped on the jersey. "I wanted the stage victory. The only thing that counts is going across the line with your arms up."

Slowly he discovered the charm of the leader's jersey. Alone in yellow, the leader is easy to spot as the pack shoots by in a hum of spokes and the spectators' shouts of 'Allez.' Before each morning's start, who can a fan more want to be photographed with than the man in the yellow jersey? The attention seduced him and he warmed to his new role.

Who is this Barteau? the fans asked, knowing only that he was a second-year professional for Renault in his first Tour. "I'm happy and spontaneous," he explained. "If I hadn't become a bicycle racer, I would have joined the circus. I'm just kidding. I kid about a lot of things, but when it comes to cycling, I'm serious." As a boy he played soccer and ran cross-country but turned to cycling because that was the family heritage. His father, Henri, who had also been his coach, had been an amateur rider of some distinction in Normandy, and so had been Vincent's two older brothers and an uncle. Between 1974 and 1982, Barteau won 200 races, was three times champion of Normandy in different age categories and the French junior champion in 1980. "But when you become a pro," he said, "none of that counts. You start at zero."

Barteau well remembered his first victory in the Normandy championship. "I was in high school, learning to become a furnace repairman in Caen, 7 A.M. to 7 P.M., and I was bored. One day in 1976 I was looking out the window and watching the sun and the grass, and I just wanted to get outside. So in the middle of class I packed my briefcase and left. The teacher said, 'Where are you going, Barteau? You'll be sorry.' I couldn't help myself. I went home by bus, got on my bike, rode 100 kilometers and said to myself, 'How am I going to explain this to my father?' But he was great. He just said, 'Let's start getting ready for the championships.' And two weeks later I was the champion."

With his snub nose and open, almost insolent, face, Barteau resembles the fresh kid — the wise guy — who sat in the back of everybody's high school class and sassed the teacher. In the yellow jersey, he got away with it. Since 1984, though, he had bounced from team to team: Renault, RMO, ADR and now Castorama. He was a good friend of Greg LeMond, with whom he had shared a room during their young days, and LeMond looked after him, inviting him on visits to the United States, lending him his car and sometimes finding a place for him on his current team.

In 1989, with his glory days past, Barteau won the stage of the Tour that every French rider yearns for, the one on July 14, Bastille Day. He pumped his fists enthusiastically as he coasted across the finish line in Marseille and spent the rest of his time there beaming in happiness.

That wasn't cool and Barteau likes to think that he is, above all else, cool. It was time to redress his image. Mont St. Michel? "It's beautiful, I agree, but who cares?"

Chapter 11
_____ A Long Day in the Rain

There was more rain ahead, seven hours of heavy and steady rain, when the Tour passed its longest day, 301 kilometers from Avranches to Rouen. By coincidence it was July 4 and Normandy — with its many memorials to D-Day and the battles of World War II — seemed the perfect spot to celebrate the holiday. Avranches itself was liberated by General George Patton's troops, and one of their tanks stood guard outside the town so near the invasion beaches. Multinational 7-Eleven remembered its roots and flew American flags from the team car during the fifth stage.

The holiday mood didn't last long, even allowing for traditional French reluctance to admit that no French troops landed at D-Day or for weeks afterward. At kilometer 35, as the road turned away from the English Channel at Granville, Henri Manders of the Helvetia team attacked. He was quickly joined by Bruno Cornillet of Z, Jean-Claude Colotti of RMO, Patrick Tolhoek of Buckler, Giancarlo Perini of Carrera, Dag-Otto Lauritzen of 7-Eleven and Jesper Skibby of TVM. With the wind at their backs, they soon built a lead approaching six minutes. To some teams in the pack it must have felt like *déja vu* of the first stage all over again, and the chase began.

At high speed, with many a crash in its wake, the pursuit continued for an hour. Later, members of the Castorama team admitted they had known what was coming.

"You didn't have to be very smart to guess it," said Thierry Marie. He should have been in a holiday mood too, since the race had passed close enough to his home to allow him to become one of the day's 'regionals' and to greet his family and friends. Marie, though, was wan.

"For Laurent to feel better, the weather had to be good, the stage had to be short and the riders had to set a moderate pace. Instead it rained, the stage was 300 kilometers long and everybody rode like crazy. And so ..."

And so, nearing St. Lô at kilometer 90, Laurent Fignon drifted over to his team car and said simply to his coach, Cyrille Guimard, "I'm stopping in the feed zone," 20 kilometers ahead. Guimard answered tersely, "Warn the boys."

Three-quarters of an hour later, at Villers Bocage, as the rain continued to pelt down, Fignon slowed, turned his bicycle around and left the Tour. He found a Castorama team car, climbed in and was driven to the night's hotel in Rouen.

Teammate Vincent Barteau was another regional. At Bellengreville, two kilometers from his home near Caen, he had stopped to be welcomed by his father, his wife, their two children and a handful of his fans. This was at kilometer 163, an hour after Fignon quit, and Barteau went unhappily through the ritual.

"Laurent told me yesterday that his calf was hurting. I didn't think this morning that he would be going far. He was in pain, his morale was shot, it was raining and we had 300 kilometers to cover. And so...."

And so, once again, Fignon had quit the Tour. This marked the third time, after 1986 and 1988. Of all the jinxes that bedeviled Fignon, the strangest seemed to be that he could not finish a Tour that moved clockwise around the country; when he won in 1983 and 1984, the direction was counterclockwise.

The news of his setting foot to ground and delivering his *dossard* number to the officials spread quickly through the pack. Minutes later, just after the feed zone, the seven breakaways were caught and the tempo slowed. Not until kilometer 206, near Lisieux, was there another attack, with Gerrit Solleveld of the Buckler team off to take his chances. He got as far as 9 minutes 30 seconds ahead before the pack awakened and whittled five minutes away. The Dutchman was an easy winner of the stage, but the headlines belonged to Fignon.

A Problem of Attitude

All Gaul is divided into three parts concerning Laurent Fignon: those who don't like him, those who don't like him but are willing to overlook their feelings as long as he wins, and those who don't like him but are willing to overlook their feelings as long as he loses.

The third group is by far the largest, and reached cult proportions when Greg LeMond made up a 50-second deficit and defeated Fignon by eight seconds to win the 1989 Tour on its final day. "You should see the mail I received, all the nice things people had to say," Fignon reported. Even President François Mitterrand, a keen follower of bicycle racing, sent a letter of condolence, the contents of which Fignon refused to divulge.

The headline on a provincial French newspaper in April said it all: "Fignon Alone Against Everybody." Although the paper was talking about the Paris–Roubaix race, its headline summed up the complex rider who was a national hero after he first won the Tour de France in 1983 and an embarrassment after he won it again in 1984. Since then he has only strengthened his reputation as a man respected but not admired, a rider who battles friend and foe alike.

By attacking a teammate, Thierry Marie, to win the Tour of Holland over him by one second in the summer of 1989, Fignon squandered the sympathy he had generated a month before on the Champs-Élysées. The script was familiar: The year before he had attacked another teammate, Gerard Rué, to edge him for victory in the Tour of the European Community. "I like to win," Fignon often says. "I'm a winner." Piling it on a few weeks after the Tour of Holland, Fignon attacked another rider on the French national team, Thierry Claveyrolat, in the world championship road race, enabling LeMond to win.

Was Fignon repentant? Not at all. Does he deign to admit a mistake? Never. After he proved positive in a drug test in the 1989 World Cup team time trial, Fignon refused any explanation except to say that laboratories were not infallible.

94

"The charges don't touch me personally," he said. "I prefer to disregard them." 'His attitude,' the French say with a shrug, the problem has always been his attitude.

In 1983 it was still marginally acceptable for Fignon to celebrate his first victory in the Tour by trading in his Renault car — "Everybody drives one of these," he said with a sniff, to the disapproval of both a public that couldn't afford his model and of his team sponsor, the same Renault — for a Ferrari. "I always promised myself one. I like speed."

Treading the same borderline, Fignon spent the winter at a long round of night-club appearances. *Le tout Paris* — the swells of the capital — had embraced the young man with blond bangs, granny glasses and the reputation of being professional bicycling's intellectual on the basis of a year in veterinary college and an appetite for Stephen King novels. Did Eddy Merckx, the self-appointed keeper of the sacred flame of the sport's tradition of asceticism, complain that Fignon was a playboy? "Merckx? Who's he?" Fignon retorted. "I don't know any Merckx."

Fignon was only 23 years old, people said in his defense. He had been little more than an unproven support rider until the Renault team's leader, Bernard Hinault, developed knee tendinitis and had to sit out the 1983 Tour, opening the door for his teammate. In his unexpected glory, Fignon was entitled to mouth off, especially against Merckx, who is, after all, a Belgian. Frenchmen are always contemptuous of Belgians.

The next year, after he dominated the Tour and crushed Hinault, now riding for La Vie Claire, Fignon went too far. This time he mocked a fellow Frenchman. In a brash attempt to win that Tour, Hinault attacked during the climb to Alpe d'Huez and was easily overtaken and passed by Fignon, who later said, "When Hinault took off, he made me laugh." The quote is still thrown in his face by reporters who might have had little good to say about Hinault personally but could not bear to see a hero of the sport ridiculed.

As he grew older, Fignon's few defenders found other explanations for his coldness. One was the death of his closest and nearly only friend in the pack, Pascal Jules, in a car crash in 1987. Afterward, when he was asked about complaints that his teammates didn't know him and were unable to get close to him, Fignon snapped, "They're paid to ride for me, not to be my friends."

Another explanation was his realization that he was not Superman, as he seemed to be when he won the 1984 Tour by more than 11 minutes, but just another vulnerable body in a dangerous sport. He developed tendinitis in his left heel in 1985 and, despite sporadic successes, did not really make it all the way back until 1988.

Revealingly, after LeMond was shot and nearly killed in a hunting accident in 1987, Fignon was the only European rider who sent him a message of condolence. So he is capable of sensitive gestures as well as arrogant ones. But the arrogant ones are plentiful: In the 1989 Giro d'Italia, Fignon turned his head so often whenever press photographers appeared that they complained they had nothing to show of him except his ponytail. In the 1989 Tour he was awarded the Prix Citron, the Lemon Prize, by photographers for his lack of cooperation. He rarely grants interviews and, if they are held in his home in Paris, he charges for the privilege. As one of the very few French stars in professional cycling, he is under intense pressure, but the evidence has mounted that the real explanation for Fignon's behavior is that he is a boor.

In the spring of 1990 he recorded two important victories that said much about him and his career: A week after he finished first in the Critérium International, he won a court case brought by a television cameraman who charged that a kick in the stomach from Fignon had caused a rupture. The evidence supporting the cameraman's claim was not overwhelming, a judge ruled.

Neither triumph changed Fignon's public behavior or the self-defensive way he has spoken since that fateful last stage of the 1989 Tour. True, LeMond won the Tour and the world championship road race that year, but Fignon remained unimpressed. "It was my year," he insisted, citing his victories in the Giro, Milan–San Remo, the Tour of Holland and the

36. Right: Fabio Parra displays the lamb awarded to his Kelme team by protesting farmers as a goodwill gesture. (photo Presse-Sports)

37. Below: A team mechanic clears away wool caught on spare bicycles when the Tour made its way through roadblocks set up by sheep raisers. (photo Presse-Sports)

38. Left: Moreno Argentin on his way to victory in the third stage. (photo Cor Vos)

39. Below: Gianni Bugno, winner of the 1990 Giro and leader of the Italian Renaissance. (photo Presse-Sports)

40.
Right:
Eric Van
Lancker
of
Panasonic
is down
after one
of many
crashes
in the
early
going.
(photo
Cor Vos)

41. Below: Gerard Rué, the regional, stops to chat with relatives in Brittany on the fourth stage. (photo Presse-Sports)

42. Above: A Tour doctor tries to help a Seur rider after a crash. But Roque de la Cruz had to be hospitalized. (photo Presse-Sports)

43. Below: The American-based 7-Eleven team flew the colors on the 4th of July, the Tour's fifth stage. (photo Presse-Sports)

44. Above: The Tour passes a town in Normandy that still celebrates its liberation in 1944 by American tank forces. (photo Presse-Sports)

45. Below: Riders approach the finish of the fourth stage at Mont St. Michel. (photo Presse-Sports)

46. Above: Buckler team coach Jan Raas helps Jelle Nijdam after a flat on the fifth stage. (photo Presse-Sports)

47. Below: Laurent Fignon, Tour winner in 1983 and 1984, trails the pack in the fifth stage. (photo Presse-Sports)

48. Above: In the feed zone, Fignon turns around and quits the 1990 Tour. (photo Cor Vos)

49. Below: Fignon climbs into his Castorama team car, leaving the Tour behind. (photo Presse-Sports)

50. Above: Gerrit Solleveld on his way to the Buckler team's second victory, on the fifth stage. (photo Cor Vos)

51. Below: Tour riders board a plane to travel from Normandy in the north-west of France to Lorraine in the north-east. (photo Presse-Sports)

52. Right: More rain awaits the riders at the other end of the country. (photo Presse-Sports)

53. Below: A weary Raul Alcala talks to Jonathan Boyer after the time trial, stage seven. (photo Presse-Sports)

54. Left: Olaf Ludwig lofts the wheel of cheese that was one reward for his victory in the eighth stage. (photo Cor Vos)

55. Below: Two of the best young Soviet riders: Dmitri Konichev, left, and Slava Ekimov. (photo Presse-Sports)

56. Above: During the 10th stage, the pack heads for the first mountains of the 1990 Tour. (photo Presse-Sports)

57. Below: Greg LeMond rides shoulder to shoulder with teammate Ronan Pensec, protecting him on the mountainous 10th stage. (photo Presse-Sports)

58. Left:
Ronan
Pensec
acknow-
ledges the
crowd's
applause
after he
donned
the yellow
jersey on
Mont
Blanc.
(photo
Cor Vos)

59. Below: Thierry Claveyrolat climbing to the stage victory on
Mont Blanc. (photo Presse-Sports)

60. Right: Roger
Zannier, the sponsor
of Pensec's Z team,
after the Frenchman
took the yellow
jersey. (photo
Presse-Sports)

61. Below: On the
way to Alpe d'Huez in
the 11th stage.
(photo Presse-Sports)

62. Next page: The
Tour dwarfed by the
Alps on the 11th
stage. (photo
Presse-Sports)

63. Above: Stephen Roche crosses the Glandon. (photo Cor Vos)

64. Below: Alpe d'Huez provides room among tens of thousands of Dutchmen for some Italians too. (photo Presse-Sports)

65. Next page: Up, up, and up the hairpin turns comes the pack. (photo Presse-Sports)

Grand Prix des Nations, his second place in the Tour de France, fourth place in the Tour of Romandie, sixth place in the world championship and seventh place in Liège–Bastogne–Liège. In FICP points, he overhauled Sean Kelly and Charly Mottet and moved briefly into first place in the computerized rankings of the world's best 600 professionals. "Where does LeMond rank?" he asked rhetorically. (Fifth then.)

In consistency, Fignon was also impressive. LeMond crammed his season into two dazzling months, but Fignon's top showings extended from the opening classic of Milan–San Remo in March to the Grand Prix des Nations in October.

All of this Fignon carefully recited. "Everybody says that LeMond was the rider of the year, and that irritates me," he complained to *l'Équipe*. "He's a very good racer, very difficult to beat. But he put it together for only two months, and I did it all year long. The rider of the year — and I say it without false modesty — wasn't him. Starting in March, I won a big race every month except April. For anybody, that's a really exceptional season."

Convinced? Neither were the French.

Chapter 12
_____ Starting Over in the East

Of the 195 riders left in the Tour, only Eddy Planckaert refused to fly the next day on a chartered jet covering the 585 kilometers from Deauville in Normandy to Sarrebourg in Lorraine. Like the team mechanics, journalists and officials who followed the race in cars, Planckaert drove the distance, surrendering to his fear of flying. It was a boring trip across the north of France, the Belgian reported later, but better five or six hours of boredom than the cold sweat and terrible dizziness he had known the two times in his life he had been in a plane.

He missed little aboard the jet except a chance to participate in what had become the popular game of estimating Steve Bauer's chances of keeping the yellow jersey. The riders were badly split, but few gave Bauer better than a 50-50 outlook. Bernard Hinault and Cyrille Guimard were less sanguine: Each said 30 percent. "If he didn't have those 10 minutes, I'd give him no chance," Guimard said. "But 10 minutes, that's an awful lot to take back. Anyway, I give LeMond 50 percent."

More and more people were favoring LeMond now, despite the 10 minutes. LeMond himself refused to discuss either his own or Bauer's chances, but the Canadian was not as reticent. For all his brave talk, he admitted that he was not underestimating his neighbor, former teammate and training partner. "You know," he joked after the Futuroscope breakaway, "10 minutes between Greg and me, that's a lot. But 10 minutes between me and Greg, that's not so much."

Now, nearly a week later, he looked seriously at his chances. "I can't give you a number," he said. "But if I didn't believe in myself to the maximum, I wouldn't have any chance. I've got to believe. Last year, in the last time trial, everybody gave Fignon 90 percent and LeMond 10. Only LeMond gave himself a 100 percent chance to win."

So the time passed on the flight in joking and nervous conversation. The riders seemed to turn sullen when they reached the eastern part of the country and saw that it was raining there too. Rain and narrow roads and a few unskillful bike handlers had added up to harrowing crashes nearly every day so far.

The next day, on the sixth stage, 202.5 kilometers from Sarrebourg to Vittel in the Vosges region, tempers were so frayed that Eric Van Lancker, the winner of Liège–Bastogne–Liège, lost his self-control and cursed and then tried to punch a Colombian, Martin Farfan, who seemed to be in the middle of many pile-ups. The Colombians had long been ridiculed for their clumsiness, but a new target was the Soviet team that competed for Alfa Lum.

"They don't know anything, they still ride as if they're amateurs," complained Laurent Biondi of Histor-Sigma. Scorn was directed equally at the erratically driven Alfa Lum team car, which had bumped Luc Leblanc, a French rider, on the way to Rouen. When Leblanc went down, he caused a dozen others to crash too. Among them was Moreno Argentin, who was so badly hurt that he had not started the stage to Vittel. Beset by strong winds and intermittent rain, the pack had two more crashes, one of them putting Ronan Pensec on the road. "It would be pretty dumb to lose everything because of a crash," he said ruefully as his minor injuries were treated. At the finish, it was time for the sprinters, and five of the best fought it out before Jelle Nijdam of Buckler edged Jesper Skibby of TVM and Johan Museeuw of Lotto.

More meaningfully, a bit of history was made on the second and last small hill of the stage. When Dmitri Konichev of Alfa Lum passed first over the Flye hill, he gained five points toward the best climber's jersey and moved ahead of Claudio Chiappucci, 33 points to 30, in the standings. For the first time in the history of the Tour de France, a Russian was in a leader's jersey.

Nice Guys Finish Second

The Buckler team was celebrating its third stage victory in six days of the Tour. First there was Frans Maassen in the Futuroscope breakaway, then Gerrit Solleveld on the road to Rouen and now Jelle Nijdam in Vittel. Like the first two riders, Nijdam was happy to share the credit. Nodding toward Jan Raas, the Buckler coach, Nijdam said, "There's the man who's taught me how to think and race. He's taught me that you must always decide how strong everybody else is and that the time just before the sprint is as important as the sprint itself. The only thing he hasn't taught me is how to get rid of my bad habit of always turning around 20 meters from the line to see where the others are."

Nijdam could afford to poke fun at himself: This was his fifth stage victory in the Tour since 1987, an impressive showing, except that it was only half as many as Raas won a decade earlier with Panasonic.

Another team official had helped Nijdam too in the last few years. That was Joop Zoetemelk, whose legs and pride told him, at age 41 in 1987, that it was time to retire as a rider. Zoetemelk obeyed, reluctantly. "Can you see me behind a counter selling sporting goods?" he asked plaintively before deciding to stay on as a team official.

Like the man himself, his farewell to the sport was international. The first celebration was staged in Germigny l'Éveque, some 50 kilometers east of Paris, where hundreds of fans ignored a cold rain to attend a cyclocross race in his honor in the French village where the Dutch-born Zoetemelk has lived for nearly two decades. Then came a trip to Tokyo to allow Japanese fans their last — and first — look at him. Following that, another last race was held in the Paris suburb of Montreuil, whereupon Zoetemelk went to say farewell at the six-day race in Maastricht, the Netherlands, and at a cyclocross near Amsterdam.

All the year amounted to a farewell tour for the veteran rider, who spent the season making the rounds in France, Belgium and the Netherlands, carefully choosing races to avoid the tough ones. Despite his fabled dedication to training and the spartan life, Zoetemelk had reached the point where he could no longer keep up with the pack, which averaged 15 years younger than he was.

How difficult was it to let go? "When I was younger," he said, "I thought it would be easy to live without a bicycle. And now I'm terrified of stopping. I think that as long as I have the strength to do well, I'll stay. It's as simple as that."

Or not so simple. For the first time since 1974, when he was seriously injured, Zoetemelk did not ride in the Tour de France in 1987. "The day the Tour de France goes off without me," he had said a few years earlier, "that's when I'll feel old." His absence ended his record of 16 appearances and finishes in the Tour.

Nice guys finish second — Zoetemelk did that six times, also a record, in the Tour. He won just once, in 1980, when Bernard Hinault had to yield the yellow jersey because of tendinitis in a knee.

Zoetemelk's misfortune was to bridge the era between Eddy Merckx, who won the Tour five times starting in 1969, and Hinault, who won five times beginning in 1978. The Dutchman was second in 1970, '71, '76, '78, '79 and '82. Still, his victories were impressive: the 1968 Olympic gold medal in the team time trial; Dutch road champion in 1971 and '73; a handful of classics; the Vuelta in 1979 and the world championship in 1985, when he was 38 and by three years the oldest professional champion ever in the road race. Typically, when he crossed the finish line, he started to raise his arms in the traditional claim of victory before quickly pulling them down. "The moment I crossed the line and raised my arms, I wondered, 'Is there anyone ahead that I didn't see break away?' " Caution was always Zoetemelk's watchword.

When he was a boy in the village of Rijpewering, near Leiden, this adage hung in his home: "Do not praise the day before the evening comes." Endurance and patience were the keys to Zoetemelk's personality, a psychologist said. "He is the kind of person who knew all along that the snail would win in Aesop's fable," the psychologist wrote in a cycling magazine.

Zoetemelk's father, a farmer, offered the magazine *Miroir du Cyclisme* another view of his son's personality: "He wasn't even 12 years old when I asked him to dig a hole with a shovel in the garden and told him I'd say when it was deep enough. I forgot all about it and when I got home that evening, the hole was so deep that we had to lift him out because he couldn't have climbed out alone. It can seem stupid, but for me it was a sign of his character."

He showed his character again in 1987, when he threatened to sue international cycling authorities if they did not waive the rule that nobody over 40 could compete. The waiver was granted.

But character did not explain it all. In 1974, Zoetemelk rounded a corner in the Midi Libre race in France and collided at high speed with a car parked where it shouldn't have been. His skull was fractured and the injury led to spinal meningitis, which nearly killed him. After eight months of physical inactivity, the doctors said he had recovered but would need at least five years to regain his strength. Instead, he started the next season with a victory in his first major race, Paris–Nice.

His seriousness as a racer was acclaimed. "Joop doesn't have any secret except to remain faithful to the most simple and most healthy principles," said Raas, his coach with Superconfex. "He's always led a calm life. Nothing bothers him. He sacrifices everything to racing, but to him it isn't a sacrifice."

The sacrifices over, Zoetemelk had no particular plans for the future. He and his wife own a hotel in the city of Meaux, near his village, but he did not become overly involved in running it. Nor could this quiet man imagine a career in sports broadcasting. He seemed happiest as a public relations representative for Buckler, traveling to races, spreading goodwill and continuing, years later, to make his farewells.

102

A Long Time Trial

On paper Greg LeMond was the overwhelming favorite in the 61.5-kilometer time trial over rolling country between Vittel and Épinal. Nobody could forget the first and similar time trial the year before, 73 kilometers from Dinard to Rennes in Brittany, where LeMond unveiled his triathlete handlebars and stormed to a 24-second victory to show that at last, more than two years after he lay bleeding nearly to death, he was back among the premier riders. Better, he was ahead of them, taking 24 seconds from Pedro Delgado, 56 seconds from Laurent Fignon, 2:16 from Erik Breukink, 2:50 from Steve Bauer, 5:03 from Raul Alcala and 7:07 from Ronan Pensec.

That was all down on paper, but the Épinal time trial was ridden on the road. Moreover, on a road that was dry for most of the field and treacherously wet for the leaders, who set off at the end, in reverse order of standing. A cold and overcast day predictably turned to rain on the seventh stage.

All was well at the first timing, kilometer 20, where the American recorded 24 minutes 45 seconds. That translated into the fastest clocking so far, 12 seconds ahead of the previous best, set by Miguel Indurain of the Banesto team. The Basque had maintained his pace and led those riders already finished, including Gianni Bugno, who was down 23 seconds, and Delgado, down 41 seconds.

When he heard his time, LeMond was pleased. He was following the same strategy he had used into Rennes: "I paced myself to go faster at the end." It made sense until the moment that Alcala passed the same checkpoint and was timed in 24 minutes flat.

From then on, it was better to throw away the paper left from the year before. LeMond rode strongly but kept losing time to Indurain, Bugno and Delgado; Alcala rode far more strongly and kept gaining time on the leaders. At the 41-kilometer checkpoint, LeMond was only the ninth fastest so far, two minutes behind Indurain, while the Mexican was 1:22 ahead of the leader. "At the halfway point I was told that I was one and a half minutes ahead of the others," Alcala said.

"I knew then that I had the stage won. I didn't take any risks after that. I didn't want to crash."

He and LeMond were cautious on the descent into Epinal, taking the seven tight and wet turns more slowly than those who rode on dry roads. At the finish, Alcala had a comfortable lead of 1:24 on Indurain, in second place. Third was Bugno, who was beginning to show his Giro form. LeMond was fifth, 2:11 back. If he was disappointed, he refused to admit it. "I feel I was second on the stage because Indurain and the others rode on dry roads," he insisted. "Of all the guys who had to ride in the rain, only Alcala beat me."

LeMond admitted that he was not surprised to be beaten by the Mexican. What did surprise him, he continued, was that Pensec had labored in only 15 seconds behind him. Bauer had done well too, finishing 14th, or 2:43 behind Alcala, but Pensec — never a time trialer — had halved the Canadian's lead by finishing seventh, 2:26 behind. The Frenchman, who left two minutes ahead of Bauer, had expected to be overtaken and asked Z's assistant *directeur sportif*, Serge Beucherie, to blow the horn of the team car when Bauer approached. He kept listening, Pensec related, and the horn never blew.

Chiappucci had done well too, finishing 15th, losing just six seconds to Bauer. The mountains were still a couple of days away and already the battle for the yellow jersey was on. All three leaders found something reassuring in their performances in the time trial. Chiappucci: "In Rennes, I lost five minutes to Bauer and here just six seconds. I've really made progress. Today I think I can say that I can win this Tour. I think I can take the yellow jersey any day now." Bauer: "I'm still in the jersey, aren't I? I'm very happy to have kept my losses down in the time trial." Pensec: "The yellow jersey is so close."

An American Pioneer

Of the 22 teams in the Tour de France, only four had all nine riders of the same nationality: Lotto was composed entirely of Belgians, Postobon of Colombians, Ariostea of Italians and Alfa Lum of Soviets. At the other end of the scale, as the sport continued to internationalize, stood three Dutch teams — Panasonic, PDM and TVM — each with riders of five nationalities. While each was predominantly Dutch and Belgian, they included Australians like Phil Anderson and Allan Peiper, Irishmen like Sean Kelly and Martin Earley, Danes like Jesper Skibby, Russians like Slava Ekimov, Mexicans like Raul Alcala, Swiss like Jorg Mueller and East Germans like Uwe Raab, Olaf Ludwig and Uwe Ampler. PDM also had an American, but he was no longer a racer.

At the Tour de Trump, a black attache case sat on the bed and the desk was littered with work papers and reports. It was a typical businessman's motel room and the typical businessman was Jonathan Boyer, a pioneer American rider in Europe.

Trim and fit at age 34, Boyer still looked like a rider. Instead, he was helping coach the PDM team in the race, and the papers on his desk dealt with the many logistical details of his job — wake-up calls, meal schedules, routes to hotels and race starts.

"It's not just sitting in the team car and deciding tactics," he explained. "It's taking care of the riders, being sure they get everything with the least amount of effort." Just then there was a knock on the door, where a Tour de Trump official stood with an invitation to PDM for a picnic dinner.

"There's always a lot of buffets in America, which is nice, but if you have a rider who's starving, he'll eat anything and then suffer in the race," Boyer said privately after promising to consider the proposal. He is a student of diet and was one of the first racers to swear off red meat and pork. "I eat chicken and fish, mostly fish," he said. As a *directeur sportif*, he continued, he does not nag his riders about not eating the wrong food. "I just make sure it's not there."

He had other objections to the picnic. "I don't like the riders' being outside, standing up, talking too much. Every ounce of energy in a stage race is vital and even talking at a press conference takes up a lot of energy."

Boyer knows. After turning professional in 1976 with the Lejeune team in France, he rode for a dozen years with a handful of other teams and competed in most major classics and stage races, including the Tour de France. In 1982 he nearly won the world championship road race; in 1983 he won a demanding mountain stage in the Tour of Switzerland, and in 1985 he finished first in the Race Across America from California to New York in just under 10 days.

"I noticed in the Race Across America that after three days I could hardly talk, because I could feel the energy I was using just talking. My energy level was so hyper-sensitive that anything — even reaching down for a water bottle and squeezing it — was energy that I had to gauge, 'Should I do it?' or 'When should I do it?' "

Looking back over his career, he noted that there was "a world of difference" between then and now. "My first pro contract was for $400 a month, and I spent half of that on rent in Paris. At the time, it actually was a good contract. Most new pros were getting a third less.

"That's certainly changed. Organization, products, bicycles — everything has changed. I was riding in wool jerseys and wool shorts. Skinsuits didn't come along until 1978 with Daniel Gisiger in the Tour of Romandie."

Boyer, a native of Moab, Utah, retired after the 1987 season, which he spent with the 7-Eleven team. Two years later the Tour de Trump began, offering American riders a showcase back home. Was Boyer sorry that by then he was off the bicycle and in the coach's car?

"Not at all," he said quickly. "I don't miss a moment of racing. I did it 18 years; I've had enough of racing. I'm doing something else I really like to do, and I can't grow unless I do something else."

Personal growth is important to Boyer, who was busily planning his future. He now lives in the Netherlands, near PDM headquarters in Maastricht, and has a small apartment in Italy, but often visits the United States on business. He feels he will return to settle there, possibly in Carmel, California, where his mother lives, or in Savery, Wyoming, where his family has owned a sheep ranch since 1905. About his other objectives he is deliberately vague, but the word 'growth' enters the conversation often.

As a racer, he had a reputation for prickliness — friendly and cooperative one minute, sullen and exasperated the next. Now he seemed mellow, direct and positive. Part of the reason was that Jock Boyer had found the success that often was elusive when he raced. In addition to his occasional coaching duties with PDM — he was the team's public relations officer during the Tour — and a post with its management, he is an importer and supplier of bicycles, components and clothing through Veltec-Boyer Sports, based in Monterey, California.

"I've been in every perspective of cycling," he said. "I've been a cyclist, on the production end, the wholesale end, the retail end, the management end and now the *directeur sportif* end. I enjoy it a lot. I really like what I'm doing."

As a teenage boy starting his career far from home, Boyer said, he felt the same enthusiasm. "I was determined to race, I loved riding," he said to explain why he left home at 17 and traveled to France to apply to a club recommended by his coach in California. "I just picked up and left home and basically didn't come back for 10 years," he said.

In 1982, while racing a heavy schedule, he began his importing business. Each job got in the way of the other, he admitted, but he persisted with both. "It was hard, but I didn't want to quit cycling and start at zero," he said. "I saw too many riders stop and all of a sudden not know what to do.

"Before two years were up, they'd used a lot of their money and ended up having bars or little bike shops." After so many years of planning, that is definitely not what Boyer foresaw in his own future.

Chapter 13
_____ Some More Firsts

In 1987, Olaf Ludwig could not get a chance to watch the Tour de France when it began in West Berlin. Although bicycle racing was a hugely popular sport in his country, East Germany refused the Tour permission to cross the Berlin Wall and begin a stage in the pertinently named Pariser Platz near the Brandenburg Gate. Nor could the Tour roll through East German territory on its way back home. The race had to fly from West Berlin to West Germany proper.

"We never saw the smallest result from the Tour in our newspapers," Ludwig remembers. "If you were interested, you had to get your information from West German radio or television. All professional sports were banned at home."

During his long and glorious career as an East German racer, Ludwig could not imagine that he would one day turn professional. "I never dreamed of it, never," he says. Nearing his 30th birthday and the winner of the 1988 Olympic road race in Seoul, he was thinking of retiring. "I would have finished my studies at the sports school in Leipzig and would have stayed in bicycling as a trainer or coach," he continues.

And then the Berlin Wall came down.

Ludwig was competing in the Sun Tour in Australia in November 1989 when he heard the news. He finished the race and returned home to Gera, East Germany, where he re-thought his position. A few days later he went to see the Minister of Sports and asked for permission to turn professional in the West. "There wasn't the slightest problem," he says, neglecting to mention that his country was falling apart and that there were bigger questions on the politicians' agendas.

Ludwig had a big question too: Could he make it in the West? "Today I received my answer," he said after the eighth stage, 181.5 kilometers from Épinal to Besançon, where Ludwig sprinted clear of a small breakaway and easily recorded the first stage victory by an East German in the Tour de France. A week previously, he had become the first East German to don a Tour leader's jersey, the green points one. Sadly, both firsts were treated with less general interest than Dmitri Konichev's winning of the mountain jersey. The reason was simply that the Soviet Union seemed destined to remain represented in the Tour de France for years to come, whereas East Germany was disappearing into a united Germany within months.

Ludwig had two goals in his first Tour de France, he said a few days before the Besançon ride. He wanted to win a stage and to wear the green jersey into Paris. They seemed humble enough for the man who had won the road race at the Olympics and the Tour de l'Avenir in France in 1983, not to mention 36 stages of the Peace Race, Eastern Europe's major race, on his way to two overall victories. For an East German, the Peace Race was as big as a race could be. Ludwig remembered how the 1972 Peace Race had passed through Gera and how he had been among tens of thousands in the city's stadium, a 12-year-old boy thrilled to watch the stage finish. On the spot he quit soccer and cross-country runing and turned to cycling, won his first two races and, five years later, joined the national team. "I've been at the top for a decade," Ludwig could truthfully say during the Tour.

He also could say that age was beginning to catch up to him. One sign was his time trial the day before. Hoping to finish in the top dozen, as he routinely did as an amateur, he had instead arrived in 131st place, an embarrassing 7:49 behind Raul Alcala. That disappointment was forgotten now as he stood on the victory podium, holding his prize of a huge wheel of cheese. "I've dreamed about a stage victory since the Tour began," Ludwig said. "I ruined my chances at Mont St. Michel by going too early, but today I settled that score."

He meant that he beat one of the few sprinters with an equal kick, Johan Museeuw of Lotto, who finished first at Mont St. Michel. In Besançon, Ludwig and Museeuw were among 13 riders who broke clear with about 10 kilometers to go. They kept their lead as the course zigzagged through the center of the city, passing four times across bridges over the Doubs River. With the line in view, Ludwig jumped ahead and had victory secure with 20 meters left.

The Tour de France, Ludwig decided, was not to be compared to the Peace Race. "The Tour is a great symphony," he said, "the Peace Race just a nice oveture."

Invasion From the East

Ask Slava Ekimov if he has any regrets about leaving the Soviet Union to join the Panasonic team in the Netherlands and the answer is yes. "I miss Russian bread," he says. "I need Russian bread."

Other than that? "No regrets. It's great. A very nice team, a very nice coach, no problems."

Ask Jan Schur if he ever expected to be able to leave East Germany to join Gianni Bugno on the Chateau d'Ax team in Italy and he says, "Why not? It's normal." Normal? So it is in a reasonable world, but what about the two decades during which the Berlin Wall snaked between East and West? And the decades of Cold War before that? "Now it's normal," Schur explained, stressing the "now."

In short, the Wall was down, the Cold War was over and the Russians were coming. Plus the East Germans and Poles. Twenty-nine East Europeans rode in the European pack in 1990, and one, Gintautas Umaras, signed with an American team, Coors Light. The emigres had an immediate impact.

Early in the season in Amsterdam, Uwe Ampler was supposed to be the star attraction at the introduction of the team sponsored by Buckler, a division of the huge Heineken brewery. At age 25, Ampler was one of the greatest amateur riders and an untouchable star of the East German juggernaut that dominated amateur cycling, road and track, for a decade. In 1986 Ampler won the world championship road race and in 1987, '88 and '89 the Peace Race.

Since the Wall opened, Ampler and five of his teammates had moved west to join professional teams. Bidding for their services was brisk and so fast-changing that, on the day Buckler expected Ampler to be the showpiece of its presentation, he was training with the rival PDM team.

The flow of Eastern European cyclists began in earnest in 1989 when the Alfa Lum team of Italy dropped all its Italian riders and replaced them with Russians. Alfa Lum fared badly in the exchange, recording only nine victories. Morale was the main problem, especially since Alfa Lum, having to pay the Soviet cycling federation $1 million for the riders, had only enough left in the budget to pay each man $200 a week.

Then too Alfa Lum was a mixture of riders either too young — Dmitri Konishev, not quite strong enough at 23 to hold off Greg LeMond in the world championship road race in 1989 — or too old — Sergei Soukhoroutchenkov, at 33 a decade past his victories in the Tour de l'Avenir and his gold medal in the road race at the 1980 Olympic Games.

The 1990 crop of recruits were mainly in their late twenties, when a rider approaches his peak years. In addition to Ampler, Ekimov and Schur, they included Joachim Halupczok and Zenon Jaskula of Poland and, from East Germany, Uwe Raab, Olaf Ludwig, Mario Kummer and Michael Huebner, the star track sprinter.

All had impressive credentials, including Ekimov's world championships in pursuit in 1985, '86 and '89, and Halupczok's victory in 1989 and Raab's in 1983 in the amateur road race at the worlds. Kummer, Schur and Ampler rode on the four-man team that won the 100-kilometer time trial at the 1988 Olympics.

"On paper they all look good," said Paul Koechli, coach of the Helvetia team in Switzerland. "But there are always questions about new professionals. Do you know, for example, how they will perform on cobblestones? Or how their morale will hold up when they no longer dominate all the races they enter? Everything will depend on how they are integrated into their teams, much more so than for a western European."

Koechli's uncertainty was generally shared as the season began.

"Capitalism isn't so easy to digest," cautioned Laurent Fignon after riding against the Eastern Europeans in a few early stage races. "The only time some of them go out on the road, it's in their big new cars." Fignon quoted Sean Kelly as having said that he had never seen riders as lazy as the Eastern Europeans. "Adapting from the amateurs to the professionals isn't easy," the Frenchman continued. "It takes devotion and patience, even for East Germans."

Cutting remarks like these were rare. More often the judges, rather than the judged, were advised to be patient. "Don't expect too much from them too soon," said Willy Tierlinck, coach of the Histor-Sigma team. "We must wait a little before judging them. They should not be expected to do well in anything more than small stage races at first." And so they did, with Ludwig especially dominating sprints, winning three stages that way in the Tour de Trump.

None of the emigres — except again at Alfa Luma, where discipline was lax — seemed daunted. Schur had to think a while when he was asked about the differences between amateur and professional racing, then said, "At the beginning of a stage, the pros ride at maybe 30 kilometers an hour and at the finish 60 kilometers an hour. For the amateurs, it's a steady 40 kilometers an hour." He reported no problems in adjusting.

Of all the Eastern Europeans, the most highly regarded were Ekimov, just 24 years old, Konichev, Ludwig and Ampler. Buckler thought it had reached agreement in principle to hire Ampler and Raab, "but they turned out to be too expensive for us," said Harrie Jansen, a Buckler official. While Ampler and Raab were still open to offers, officials of the PDM team journeyed to East Germany and landed the pair by offering about $80,000 a year to Ampler and about $50,000 to Raab. (This was a hefty pay raise, of course. Ludwig, who was reported to be earning $100,000 a year with Panasonic, has said that he was paid $800 a month as a member of East Germany's national team — $40 above an average salary. He augmented this with bonuses, such as the $20,000 he received for winning the Olympic road race. Ludwig also denied

the often-heard charge that he had been merely a professional with an amateur's license. The Peace Race, he said,
paid each rider $4,000 no matter how many stages he won
or where he finished. "I was paid like an amateur but had to
ride like a professional," he felt. "Now I'm a professional and
I'm paid like one.")

After signing Ampler, PDM insisted it had not won a
bidding war. "Ampler and Raab wanted to come with us and
money had little to do with it," said Jan Gisbers, the PDM
coach. "They rode against us in Spain and in the Tour of
Sweden last year and they said they liked the way our team
operates."

Either version was acceptable — money and prestige were
abundant among Dutch teams, which ranked first (PDM),
second (Buckler) and fifth (Panasonic) in the computerized
standings of the world's top 30 professional teams as the
season began. Their budgets reflected this: Panasonic was
spending $5.2 million at the rate of exchange then, PDM $3.7
million and Buckler $3.2 million. With this kind of money
available, PDM got Ampler and Raab and Panasonic signed
Ekimov and Ludwig; Halupczok and Jaskula went to the
Diana team in Italy, which was not competing in the Tour,
Huebner to Histor-Sigma in Belgium and Schur and Kummer
to Chateau d'Ax.

The best contract among them was won by Ekimov, who
refused to join his fellow Soviets at Alfa Lum, citing the low
pay and lack of incentive there. In the end, Panasonic gave
him $500,000, a record by far for a first-year professional.

Visiting with the Swiss

One sovereign state, the Tour, was entering another, Switzerland, and the race's police escort had to empty their holsters
at the frontier. It seemed the right metaphor to sum up the
ninth stage, 196 rolling kilometers in the Jura from Besançon
to Geneva. The Alps were starting the next day and none of
the favorites seemed eager for a shootout before then.

113

Frans Maassen had different ideas in mind. No climber, Maassen realized that this would be his last chance to wear the yellow jersey that had been so tantalizingly close since the Futuroscope breakaway. He would have liked to try to take the jersey somewhere in Brittany but had to wait, a prisoner of team strategy, while Gerrit Soleveld and Jelle Nijdam won their stages. Now team strategy changed: lacking a climber, Buckler knew this was its last chance at a stage victory until the Alps were passed.

Maassen attacked twice and twice was reeled in as 7-Eleven worked strenuously to keep Steve Bauer in the jersey one more day. At the finish, Maassen had recovered only 10 seconds of the 1:16 he needed and the Canadian was still the leader.

He knew what everybody was thinking, Bauer admitted. "I know that everybody says I could lose the jersey tomorrow in the mountains. I'm not worrying about that. I'm taking it one day at a time."

When Maassen was caught the second time, he was off the front with 19 other riders. Two of them, Eduardo Chozas of ONCE and Massimo Ghirotto of Carrera, managed to stay clear on a long descent 80 kilometers from the finish. Both are competent climbers and they used their strength to open a lead that grew to more than 40 seconds up the second category Rousses hill. Despite a sustained chase, the two were more than 1:30 ahead as they began the 22-kilometer loop around Geneva. Fighting a strong headwind, they held off all pursuit.

"Was I afraid of the Spaniard?" Ghirotto asked later. "Not at all." The Italian took the lead with half a kilometer to go and easily recorded his second victory in the Tour. He dedicated this one to his Carrera team's sponsor or, more precisely, to his sponsor's daughter, whose three-year-old daughter had been kidnapped for ransom three months before in Calabria. Ghirotto seemed to be involved in drama every time he won a Tour stage.

In the Broom Wagon

Driving in the Pyrenees in 1988, Philippe Pietrowski heard on the Tour de France's internal radio that two riders had fallen far behind. "I think we have customers," he said. "Maybe not," answered Raymond Guilmin, sounding hopeful. "Maybe not."

Pietrowski and Guilmin spent their days with the race in the *voiture balai*, or broom wagon, trailing the field to pick up riders who have quit. The symbol of their work is the 15-foot-long broom — a *balai* — mounted atop their blue 12-seat van. "We sweep up after the race," Pietrowski explained before the 163-kilometer stage from Blagnac to the mountain resort of Guzet Neige. The stage was expected to generate business for the broom wagon. It travels third from the end of the nearly 1,000 cars, trucks, motorcycles and, of course, bicycles in the Tour. Behind it come only a flatbed truck for wrecked cars and a police van marked *fin de course*, or end of the race.

So far back does the broom wagon roll that neither Pietrowski nor Guilmin came within 15 minutes of seeing the finish of a stage. When Massimo Ghirotto of Carrera won the day's climb, for example, the men in the broom wagon learned about it only by listening to a commercial radio station that broadcast the finish live. The men in the van only heard how, just before the sprint finish, Philippe Bouvatier of the BH team and Robert Millar of Fagor misunderstood a policeman's hand signal, began to take a wrong turn down a side road 400 meters from the line and were barely beaten by Ghirotto after they swerved back onto the course. It was a rare and exciting finish but neither of the Frenchmen in the van minded not being there. "We don't miss much — just seeing it happen," Guilmin remarked.

When a rider quits the race, he usually stops at the side of the road and waits for the broom wagon to arrive, although a star rider — like Laurent Fignon in rainswept Brittany — is often allowed to enter one of his team's two cars. In either case, Pietrowski helps hang the rider's bicycle on an accompanying truck and Guilmin performs the symbolic act of

115

removing the numbers each rider wears for identification.

"I try to comfort them when they get into the van," Guilmin said. "I tell them what a hard race the Tour de France is, and I always say that a lot of other riders have quit too. I also tell them to think of next year, when they'll have another chance.

"Sometimes I help, sometimes not. I've seen riders weeping while they sit in the van and I've seen some laughing with relief that it's over. Most just sit there, quiet and exhausted."

If the van becomes too crowded, as it sometimes does in the highest mountains, the overflow is moved to the flatbed truck carrying the bicycles. Or riders may be let out at a feeding station, where soigneurs eventually drive them to their hotels.

Pietrowski, then 26 years old, had been driving the van for two years and Guilmin, then 67, had been a passenger for four years. He was a *commissaire*, or race official, and had spent 18 years riding second seat on a motorcycle, looking for infractions. "Then I got too old and they put me here," he said. He is a softspoken, grandfatherly man who gave the impression that he might be willing to overlook minor transgressions. As he said while the van rolled past fields green with corn and golden with sunflowers, "No bicycle race in the world is as hard as this one. And a commissaire's job is hard too. He must use his judgment."

The van never moves up the long parade to seek out a lagging rider but, if the last rider drops to the very rear, the van will remain a few feet behind him. To some, that might suggest a shark trailing a shipwreck survivor on a raft, but that impression is false, Guilmin insisted. "They recognize that we're not looking for business," he said. "It doesn't please us to have to pick somebody up."

He made his point when the Tour radio announced that No. 127, Atle Kvalsvoll, a Norwegian with the Z team, had fallen far behind on the climb to the Agnes pass. A few minutes later, Kvalsvoll came into sight as he labored up the mountain, 1,595 meters high and rated first category in difficulty and steepness. Then a first-year professional who was far down in the general classification, Kvalsvoll was struggling at a pace that registered less than 5 kilometers an hour on the van's speedometer. For a few minutes his team car rode alongside him to offer encouragement while a mechanic poured water on his head to help on the sunny and blazingly hot climb, but still Kvalsvoll wobbled. Even the cheers of the spectators did not help him push the pedals faster.

"Is he the last rider?" a spectator shouted at Guilmin. He looked away and quickly nodded yes, as if he were afraid of embarrassing the rider with an answer he might hear.

When a panel announced that the Norwegian still had 10 kilometers of climbing before the finish, the radio in the van was reporting Ghirotto's bizarre victory high atop the mountain. Kvalsvoll was fighting not only to finish but also to finish within the specified time differential with the winner. Beyond that point, which is determined by a complicated formula, he could be eliminated even if he did finish.

"I'm worrying about the time delay," Guilmin said to Pietrowski.

Then spectators began to take turns pushing the rider up the long series of switchbacks as Guilmin looked on. For a commissaire, pushes — even unsolicited — are exactly the sort of infraction to be on guard against, and indeed Kvalsvoll was later penalized 300 francs and 40 seconds for four unsolicited pushes.

Whatever the number above four, Kvalsvoll must have broken the Tour de France record. One at a time, two at a time and sometimes even three at a time, fans planted their hands on his back and shoulders and on his bicycle seat and sped him up the mountain. Finally he crossed the finish line, in last place, 32 minutes 21 seconds behind the winner.

"Was he within the time limit?" Guilmin anxiously asked a finish-line judge who climbed into the parked van at the end. Assured that Kvalsvoll had been, Guilmin smiled: No riders had entered the van on this stage, the first and easier of two in the Pyrenees.

But, he said gloomily, "Tomorrow we'll be busier."

Chapter 14
_____ In the Alps

Ronan Pensec celebrated his 27th birthday with as pretty a present as the Tour de France can offer: the Frenchman received the yellow jersey. "It's a nice gift, for sure," he said as he stood on the victory podium after the 118.5-kilometer climb from Geneva to St. Gervais-Mont Blanc and slipped into the jersey. He looked dapper for someone who usually dresses in the rocker mode, verging on punk, and is so cool that he wore his sunglasses atop his head during a 10th stage ridden in strong sun and blustery winds.

Climbing strongly as the Tour began its stay in the Alps, Pensec easily replaced Steve Bauer in the overall lead. With his triumph and the 10-minute lead over most favorites that he gained at Futuroscope, Pensec established himself as a strong contender for the final victory. That, of course, was also what people had said about Bauer.

Pensec had a little help from his friends on the way to his birthday party. The Z team kept the pace high up to the final eight-kilometer assault of the Bettex ski resort on Mont Blanc. Up to that point, Bauer had managed to hang on in a large group of riders, including Pensec. But with six kilometers left, Pedro Delgado attacked twice, carrying with him most of the favorites, including Raul Alcala and therefore Pensec. "Stay with Alcala and don't worry about Bauer — he's cooked," Greg LeMond had advised Pensec early in the final climb.

LeMond had it right. After falling behind on the first of three peaks, the Canadian made up his deficit on the descent and stayed with the favorites' group on the second climb. By the third and final mountain, he could no longer respond. "When Delgado and Pensec attacked, I simply couldn't stay with them," Bauer reported. "I thought it better to climb at my own pace and lose the time than try to stay with them and explode."

His own pace proved far too slow. Pensec's lead on the climb jumped from seven seconds to 28 in two kilometers and to 45 seconds in another kilometer. At the finish, Pensec had far overcome his 17-second deficit at the start, crossing the line 1:38 ahead of Bauer, who fell to third place overall, 1:21 behind. Second, 50 seconds behind Pensec, was Claudio Chiappucci.

Bauer was disappointed and relieved at the same time. Finally the pressure was off. "I've accomplished more than I ever hoped for," he said. "Ten days in the yellow jersey is really something, the best thing in my life." Trying to sound upbeat, Bauer added that he had at least remained on the three-man victory podium. "Let me finish second in the Tour and I'll be happy."

While Pensec was the big winner, the first rider across the line was Thierry Claveyrolat, a Frenchman with the RMO team. He slipped away early and finished 1:53 ahead of Uwe Ampler, an East German with PDM, and Charly Mottet, another Frenchman with RMO. Claveyrolat and Mottet are both natives of the region in eastern France and know its mountains well. "It's not Alpe d'Huez, but it's on the way there," LeMond said, sounding a little worried about how he would do in the highest Alps. "I wasn't super," he admitted. "I'm not at 100 percent, something's missing. Or maybe it's that I'm a little lower than last year and so many other riders are a little higher."

He found himself in the unenviable position of having to defend his teammate rather than going off on his own behalf. While that opportunity might yet present itself if Pensec faltered, for now LeMond — the world champion and defending Tour de France champion — was simply No. 2 on the team. He knew that feeling all too well.

Back in 1985, LeMond was taught an unsparing lesson in team discipline. Bernard Hinault, then the leader of LeMond's La Vie Claire team, crashed heavily in the final 250 meters of the finish in St. Étienne, just before the Tour entered the Pyrenees. Rushed to a hospital to repair his wounds, Hinault announced, "I still have my two arms and my two legs, and

I'm far from being dead." Still, he had trouble breathing and on the climb to Luz Ardiden a few days later Hinault dropped a couple of minutes behind LeMond. Those minutes were enough to put the American in the yellow jersey on the road, the fanciful land where ambition flowers.

Scenting the real yellow jersey, LeMond pushed ahead with Stephen Roche, a rival, until the Vie Claire team car drew alongside and ordered him to help Hinault by refusing to relay Roche. "So I didn't attack," he recalled, "just rode Roche's wheel while he rested and coasted and I didn't make a move. Luis Herrera caught us and took off but still I held back, under team orders. Had I just gone with Herrera and followed him, it would have been enough to win that Tour de France for me.

"I could have won my first Tour de France that day. They told me Hinault was right behind me and even without my working with Roche, I gained a minute. From the bottom of the hill to the top, we could have taken three or four minutes out of Hinault. I coasted up that last climb. I stopped, completely stopped, and he was still a minute 13 seconds down."

Near tears and furious at the end of the stage, LeMond denounced La Vie Claire officials until he was called in for a talk. When he emerged from the high-level meeting, he was calmer. "I got a little carried away," he confessed, explaining that when he said, "This was my chance to wear the yellow jersey," he really meant only for one day before helping Hinault reclaim it.

The dispute was smoothed over, Hinault went on to win his fifth Tour and LeMond finished second, consoled by Hinault's public pledge to help the American win the next year.

All would have been well except that Hinault was unable to honor his pledge. Once the 1986 Tour started, Hinault went for the victory — not to set a record, for Hinault is sincerely uninterested in records, but because his character prevented him from not trying to win. He attacked LeMond on the road and in the press, waging physical and psychological warfare.

Conciliatory with the French press, LeMond was blunt with an American journalist, to whom he denounced Hinault late in the Tour. "He made promises to me he never intended to keep. He made them just to relieve the pressure on himself. I just wish he had said at the beginning of the Tour, 'It's each one for himself.' But he didn't, and so I rode one kind of race. If he'd said, 'It's every man for himself,' I'd have ridden differently. I have bitter feelings about him."

With no thanks to Hinault, LeMond did win the '86 Tour. It was another unsparing lesson in team discipline.

Now LeMond had a chance to show what he had learned.

First, he demonstrated that he was willing to work for Pensec by advising him to stay with Alcala and disregard Bauer. When it came to tactics, LeMond was a good man to have on your side.

Second, he was gracious to Pensec personally. "It's terrific for Ronan," he exclaimed at the team's hotel. It was also terrific for him, LeMond explained. "Tactically, we're in a perfect situation. All I have to do is watch Delgado, Bugno and Alcala. If that helps Ronan win the Tour, fine. I'm paid by Z and all we want is that a Z rider should be in the yellow jersey in Paris. If that's Ronan, swell."

At his side, Pensec was exuberant. "Pressure?" he joked. "What pressure? I've had the yellow jersey for a couple of hours now and I don't feel any pressure."

The Z team sponsor, Roger Zannier, was also celebrating a birthday, his 44th, and he was ordering champagne for everyone. The next night Zannier would scandalize traditionalists by being seen dancing in a discotheque while wearing the yellow jersey that Pensec had given him.

There was a bond between them, Pensec explained. "At the end of last year he told me that I had given him one good year out of three in the Tour. That made me think. I ride for myself but I couldn't deny that the Tour is the most important race in the year for the team. So I worked at being ready for this race."

What people sometimes forgot about Pensec was that he

121

might dress like a punk, wear his black hair in spikes and collect vintage cars and motorcycles, but he was a serious young man who had grown up, and raised his younger sister, as an orphan after their parents were killed in a car crash. "I learned young to live life," he says. Whatever Pensec was, he was no fool. "Listen," he said, "you're not going to see me announce to the world tonight that Ronan Pensec is going to win the Tour de France. All I know is that I'm going to climb Alpe d'Huez in yellow."

For the day, at least, the French had found themselves a hero. "You wouldn't be wrong in considering him a super rider," gushed Hinault in his column in *l'Équipe*. He also fielded carefully a reader's question about how the Z team should carry on — should it work for Pensec instead of LeMond?

Not at all, insisted Hinault. "I think it's more intelligent to preserve the chances of both leaders for the simple and good reason that the other favorites are now obliged to attack. Pinning all the team's chances on Pensec could help a rival rider."

The echoes of 1985 and '86 were unmistakable. If Hinault is leading, the team works for him and holds back LeMond; if LeMond is leading, Hinault attacks to make sure that they straddle the field.

"I gave my word to him that I would work for him and that's what I did," Hinault wrote in his autobiography when he discussed LeMond and the '86 Tour. "It wasn't my fault if he didn't understand how I lead a race. What I did, I did only for him. How dare he say he didn't need me to win? I spent all my time wearing out his opponents. Throughout my career I worked hard for others without having the kind of problems I had with him. Greg LeMond still has to learn the hardest lesson: humility. Humility is difficult for Americans. It seems to me that they aren't bent in that direction."

Hinault's Rules

How strange to hear a lecture on humility from Bernard Hinault, the same Hinault who often boasted as a rider, "I race to win, not to please people."

He did both constantly: won races and failed to please people.

Raymond Poulidor, 14 times a rider in the Tour and never a winner, had his favorite Hinault story, dating to his earliest days. "One understood immediately that he had character and that neither Merckx nor Poulidor impressed him. He was afraid of nothing. One day, in the Midi Libre race, I think, we started by going up a mountain. The evening before, Hinault had been hopelessly left behind and was, for all practical purposes, out of the race. But the next morning he started at full speed and stayed at the head of the pack for 25 kilometers, going all out. Behind him we had our hands full to keep up. And then, having done it and showed us, he dropped out of the race. I realized then that we were going to have further dealings with him, that he was not an ordinary racer."

Luis Ocaña, the 1973 winner of the Tour, had his own pet memory: "I remember a stage of the Dauphiné Libéré, it must have been 1975 or 1976. Everybody was calm and the pack was rolling quietly when we got to a long hill. Hinault went to the front and began to ride like a madman. I moved up to him to make him understand that this wasn't on, that he should leave the rest of us in peace. Instead of calming down, he just accelerated. We were going all out and soon were exhausted. I dropped back, but he just pushed on.

"The more everybody yelled at us from behind, the faster he went. He didn't care at all what everybody thought of him, this kid. I liked him at once."

The French call this *character*, which they admire in moderate doses. Beyond that — in Hinault's case, according to his many detractors — character soon translates into arrogance and aggressiveness.

The son of a railroad worker in the town of Yffiniac in

Brittany, Hinault seems the quintessential Breton, right down to his Celtic dark good looks. Most Frenchmen, however, do not think of these as the chief Breton trait. Instead, 'stubborn as a Breton' is a common epithet.

"People say that Bretons have a hard character, stubborn, even rude," explained Martine Hinault as she waited in their home for her husband to finish a training run over flat, windblown roads. "That's our reputation — aggressive and stubborn."

When he returned home, Hinault flopped onto the couch and politely differed. "I think it refers to people who are hard, who are able to endure a bad climate, among other things. I think when people refer to the Breton character, they mean people who, when they want something, do their best to get it."

This definition was the truth, but not the whole truth. All France was scandalized in 1982 when, a beaten man, Hinault dropped out of the one-day national championship and then, on nationwide television, blamed the public, the press and his fellow riders. The other riders kept a politic silence, but the public responded throughout the next Tour with jeers and whistles. The press let loose with long-suppressed anger. "A small masterpiece of the hateful and the stupid," judged *l'Équipe*. "In the eyes of the general public, Bernard Hinault is revealed for what he is: a great champion but a small man."

"My nature isn't always to be prudent," Hinault admitted in his living room. "As everybody knows, I can sometimes be impulsive." He laughed at his statement of the obvious.

Another word usually attached to Hinault was *méchant*, literally meaning spiteful, nasty or malicious. French homes often have signs warning of a *chien méchant*, a vicious dog. In bicycle racing, as Hinault noted, being *méchant* isn't all bad. "It's natural for a cyclist to be *méchant*," he said. "I can't understand how a racer cannot have this trait, at least a bit of it. All winners have it. People who like to fight, who like to win, they all have it. I think when you're going all out, it's impossible to do it with a smile. If you ever see me smiling during a race, you'll know I'm not really trying." Hinault's standard race photograph showed glaring, burning eyes and a set jaw. He resembled an animal on the scent and was, indeed, nicknamed for one — *le blaireau,* the badger.

Hinault rose from the couch and crossed the room to show a stuffed and mounted badger, teeth bared, that a fan had sent. "The nickname was given to me early in my career and it stuck. The badger is a strong animal, especially in relation to its small size, and he can make a lot of trouble if he's attacked. I think the nickname sort of reflects my own attitude: I can take a lot of blows without saying anything, but the next day I attack, and when I do, I can be very, very *méchant.*"

One promise Hinault did keep was to retire on his 32nd birthday, November 14, 1986. The celebration, which he had helped plan for a year, was held all day in the Breton town of Quessoy, where he lived. "It's not a funeral procession," he pledged, "but a big party."

Hinault noted the many ways he would fill his new life. He serves three months a year as a consultant to the Look sports equipment company, with which he developed the quick-release clipless pedal. With a partner, he set up a company to manufacture and market educational wooden toys for children. He also serves as a technical consultant to the Tour de France, spending one day a week in its offices and the full three weeks with the race on the road.

"I'm quitting before I'm fed up with cycling," he said. "I've seen a lot of champions who tried to hang on too long, who just couldn't do it any longer but didn't know anything else to do. Not I. It's as important for me to succeed in my new life as it was in racing."

He had no regrets, he insisted. Was the man who won 52 time trials during his career sorry that he never tried to break the record for the hour's ride? No, he said, never. When he was riding for Renault in 1979 or 1980, he continued, the team had talked about his attempting that feat and had even developed a special streamlined bicycle. Hinault's interest, however, was not in records; he liked to beat people, not time.

The feats he relished included the 140-kilometer

125

breakaway in the 1979 Tour of Lombardy, the last race of the season, that gave him the victory points to squeeze by Giuseppe Saronni for the annual Super Prestige title. Or the day in the 1977 Dauphiné Libéré when he took a curve too snug on a descent and went hurtling into a ravine, then climbed back up, remounted and won that day's stage — as well as the race itself. Or the way he recovered from an operation for tendinitis in his right knee in 1983, when the doctors gave him a 50-50 chance of ever racing again, and came back a year later to finish second in the Tour before ending his season with a fifth victory in the Grand Prix des Nations, a long time trial.

Since he turned professional in 1975, he had won more than 250 races. His trophies included the rainbow-striped jersey of the world road-race champion, which he won in 1980, the five yellow jerseys he wore at the end of the Tour, the three pink jerseys he won in the Giro, the two greenish-yellow jerseys he won in the Vuelta and the red and white striped jersey he won in the Coors Classic in Colorado in 1986. That was his final victory.

Would he miss competition? Hinault was asked. "Every day will be filled with competition now," he replied. "I've always been inspired by competition in sports and now I expect to be inspired by the competition of daily life. I don't think I'll be bored."

Thousands of fans and dozens of riders attended the retirement party, but Greg LeMond was not among them. "Are you kidding?" he responded when asked why he had not been there. For the unsparing lesson Hinault taught him in the 1986 Tour, LeMond has never forgiven his former friend and idol.

Chapter 15
_____ Where the Tour is Lost

As riders have said for decades, "The Tour is not always won at Alpe d'Huez, but is usually lost there."

Legend adds that in the early 1950s, two scouts for the Tour drove up the dirt roads to the ski resort, got out of their car near the 1,860-meter summit and stared at each other in dumb wonder. Alpe d'Huez has been on the Tour's schedule many years since then, especially in the last decade. Its roads have been graded and paved, but its 21 hairpin turns are no less terrible now than they were then, especially with at least a quarter of a million people lining the ramps, pouring water over the riders, running alongside them to shout encouragement, clapping them on the back, giving those who are struggling an illegal push. Year after year, it is the Tour's theater of high drama, and so it was once again.

Two of the leading teams had worked out precise strategy for this 11th stage, 182.5 kilometers from St. Gervais. At breakfast that morning, the Z team decided that Ronan Pensec would concentrate on staying with Claudio Chiappucci and Raul Alcala, the two best climbers closest to his yellow jersey, and Greg LeMond would watch Gianni Bugno and Pedro Delgado, the two favorites further down the general classification. If Delgado was ready to make his move, the theory went, daunting Alpe d'Huez was the place.

At the Banesto team's hotel, Delgado was indeed listening to instructions how he was to go on the offensive. The strategy was simple enough: His teammates would attack and string out the pack on the first two climbs over the 1,984-meter-high Madeleine, rated beyond category in difficulty, and the 1,950-meter-high Glandon, rated first category. Those two past, Delgado himself would do the heavy work on the way up to Alpe d'Huez.

Check? Check. After a speedy 45 kilometers in the first hour, Juan Martinez Oliver of Banesto was sent ahead along the valley leading to the Madeleine. The race exploded, breaking the pack into a lead group of 50, with 130 others strung down the mountain. When Martinez Oliver was caught with seven kilometers of the 23-kilometer climb left, Jesus Rodriguez-Magro was the next Banesto rider to attack. Then it was Miguel Indurain's turn. The Basque turned the pace even higher on the descent and reached the feed zone between the Madeleine and the Glandon more than a minute ahead of the main pursuit group.

Banesto's strategy was working, and so was Z's. Both teams were well represented at the front and LeMond was staying with Delgado until suddenly the American crashed in the feed zone while transferring his sandwiches and pastries

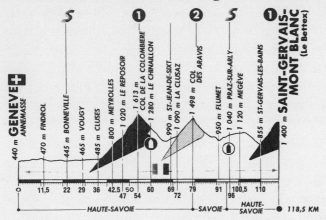

After yesterday's mountains (above), more mountains today on the stage from St. Gervais-Mont Blanc to l'Alpe d'Huez (below).

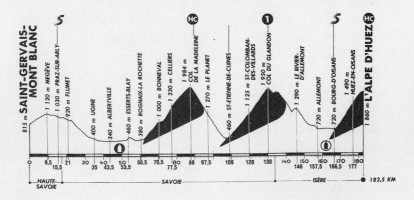

128

to his jersey pockets. "I fell on my left hand," he said later. "The middle finger was all bent at an angle and I had to pull it straight and push it back into its socket." He also had a moment of panic when he realized that he had knocked down a female spectator but her husband yelled at him, "She's OK. Get going, Greg."

He went. Up ahead, far along on the 21-kilometer Glandon climb, Indurain was being overtaken by Thierry Claveyrolat, who left the Basque more than a minute behind as he went over the peak and began to dream about his second successive stage victory in the Alps. Three and a half minutes behind the Frenchman was the main pack.

As it came down the Glandon, Delgado made his move, attacking on a steep one-kilometer rise and leaving behind most of his rivals except for LeMond and Bugno. "When Delgado went, I could have caught him," Pensec remembered. "There were only 10 meters between me and Bugno. But that wasn't our team strategy. Delgado and Bugno were for Greg to deal with. I followed our plan." Pensec stayed with Chiappucci; the second rider he was watching, Alcala, was having a bad day, the kind of bad day that loses a Tour, and was left in their dust.

Once past the short climb, the descending group picked up new speed and briefly was nearly two minutes ahead. Paced by Delgado and sometimes Bugno, the group included LeMond, Indurain, Claveyrolat and Eduardo Chozas, strong climbers all. At the foot of Alpe d'Huez, they had widened their lead to 2:30 on the Pensec group.

On the way up, Indurain was dropped first, then Chozas and then Claveyrolat. The three favorites rode together through the hairpin turns and swarms of screaming fans in what might have become the first major breakaway since Futuroscope.... Except that Bugno and LeMond refused to relay Delgado.

"I really don't understand why Bugno didn't help pull on the way up," LeMond would say at the finish. "If he had, they never would have caught us."

Delgado was equally puzzled. "Too bad it was Bugno and

LeMond who followed me on the Glandon," the Spaniard said. "Anybody else and we'd have been far gone. They never worked with me. Bugno took part in a few relays before we started up Alpe d'Huez but never again. I just don't understand."

For Bugno, it was simple. He explained later that, more than 10 minutes down on Pensec, he decided he had a lesser chance of significantly reducing the deficit than he had of winning the stage. He was not going to win the Tour de France, he understood, and preferred to save his strength and bank everything on the prestigious victory at Alpe d'Huez.

If Delgado could not understand this, he had no problem diagnosing why LeMond had not cooperated. "He played the team's game in not helping," Delgado realized. "With the yellow jersey in his team, you couldn't expect him to help."

As he had promised, LeMond was honoring team etiquette. "I just stayed on Delgado's wheel," he admitted. "But I said to myself, 'If I could work, what a day we could have.'"

Three kilometers from the top, just before the road begins to straighten and pass huge hotels, Delgado weakened and his two companions went by him. Hard behind them came a revived Claveyrolat, Abelardo Rondon of Banesto, Fabio Parra of Kelme and Erik Breukink of PDM.

At the final left turn into an uphill 300-meter finish, LeMond looked ready to record his first stage victory in this Tour. Then he swung far too wide, unable to apply pressure on his brakes because of his injured finger, and nearly clipped a steel barrier holding back spectators. As he straightened out, he realized that he was in too big a gear for the sprint but had no time to shift down. Determinedly, he launched the sprint for the line but, in the last 10 meters, Bugno passed him and finished first by less than half a wheel.

In 10th place, 48 seconds behind Bugno, Pensec kept his yellow jersey. "I've got the best team in the world," he said. "The work they did for me was fantastic." So it was, especially the role Robert Millar played in shepherding Pensec up Alpe d'Huez. "He set the perfect pace for me," Pensec said of his

Scottish teammate. "Only once or twice did I have to ask him to slow down a little. The trick was going up at my own rhythm and not forcing it. I never imagined I could make up the two minutes on Greg, Bugno and Delgado. But I never panicked. I knew that Greg wouldn't ride against me."

The winners and losers were easy to count. The foremost loser was Alcala, in 30th place for the day, 5:41 behind Bugno, and now dropped into eighth place overall. Delgado was another loser, finishing eighth and losing 40 seconds to Bugno and LeMond. His lieutenant, Indurain, lost 11:55. Steve Bauer lost 21:45 and Stephen Roche, who won the Tour so handily in 1987, lost 24:13. Faring even worse, Eric Vanderaerden, a Belgian with Buckler, was caught being towed by a team car up Alpe d'Huez and was disqualified.

The winners? Pensec, of course. Even Chiappucci, who finished 13th, losing 1:26 but staying within sight of Pensec. Claveyrolat too, with his fine fourth place and the big lead he opened on Chiappucci in the fight for the best climber's jersey. Andy Hampsten replaced Bauer as 7-Eleven's leader, finishing seventh, 40 seconds down, and moving into the top 10. Even LeMond could be counted among the winners; he had moved into third place overall. If he had not made up much time on Pensec, he had played the team game another day and gained new respect.

Breukink was another winner and could prove it. Trapped with Alcala when Delgado jumped away on the descent, the Dutchman had come back to climb Alpe d'Huez in the fastest time, 43:19 or 4 seconds better than Parra, and was awarded a gold watch worth 20,000 francs for the feat. A couple of seconds faster and Breukink could have won another honor. He finished third, a second behind Bugno and LeMond, thus missing the opportunity to become the ninth Dutchman to win the climb in 15 years.

As an old joke puts it, Alpe d'Huez is the southernmost village in the Netherlands, which lies several hundred kilometers north. The Dutch favor the village for summer vacations, especially when the Tour is dropping by, and camp out for days beforehand on the switchbacks to guarantee a good

131

seat for the race. The previous two years they had celebrated Dutch victories. In 1988, Steven Rooks, then riding for PDM, was first and a year later the winner was his close friend and teammate, Gert-Jan Theunisse.

Both had fallen far since then. Rooks, now with Panasonic, had struggled in 5:03 behind Bugno and was in 18th place overall. Theunisse wasn't even in the race. Testing positively for drugs three times in two years, he had been banned from the sport for a year.

In the Wilderness

"Even criminals are treated better than I am," Gert-Jan Theunisse complained at his home in the Netherlands. "They've stolen the bread out of my mouth. Panasonic fired me and refuses to pay my salary. Sometimes I say to myself, 'You're going crazy. Stop the fight and just start another career.' But the next day I get back on my bicycle and continue my training.

"I ride alone five or six hours every day, covering 800 kilometers a week. What keeps me going is my feeling that in the end I'll show them, I'll be back, I'll have my revenge."

He was talking to a reporter from the French newspaper *Libération* as he detailed his fight to overturn his three positive drug findings. Theunisse seemed especially bitter that his fellow riders had changed their feelings toward him. After his first conviction, during the 1988 Tour, the riders had staged a brief protest strike on his behalf. In 1990, after his second conviction, they had threatened a strike against the Giro d'Italia if he were allowed to continue competing. Attitudes were beginning to harden. Nobody bothered to warn Theunisse that team managers, responding to complaints by their riders, had gathered the night before and decided to sanction the strike.

Trembling in anger, Theunisse recalled that morning in the Giro. "All the other riders got off their bicycles and the ones closest to me said, 'We're on strike.'

" 'Me too,' I said. 'I'm with you in this strike.' I thought we were protesting about a badly lit tunnel where a bunch of the guys had crashed the day before. Then I saw that all the cameras and all the microphones were pointed at me. They were waiting for me to ride away, me, the druggy."

He was in the Giro through a loophole. When his positive finding in the Flèche Wallonne was announced in early June, he should have been suspended immediately for six months for his second conviction in three years. Instead, Theunisse and the Panasonic team learned that officials of the French Cycling Federation had not formally notified the Dutch Cycling Federation of his positive finding in the 1988 Tour. No matter that Theunisse had been penalized 10 minutes in the Tour, dropping him from fourth to 11th place, no matter that the affair had made headlines throughout Europe. The papers had never been sent, and so Theunisse technically was a first-time offender, liable only to a fine.

Embarrassing as it was to the sport, the controversy had to be settled quickly and the six-month suspension was upheld. A few days later a third positive finding, in a Spanish race, was made public and Theunisse's suspension was lengthened to a year. Panasonic then fired him for actions detrimental to its interests and image.

"That's the way this sport is," he said. "Everybody is happy only when somebody at the top is knocked down."

Had he truly been at the top? At age 27, Theunisse was not far from it. He is a gritty rider, as he proved by starting the 1989 Tour despite aching ribs that required the care of an acupuncturist on the road. Riding through his pain, the result of a crash, he scored the Alpe d'Huez victory and finished fourth overall. Major victories were expected of him and, in the free-form way the sport was developing in an era of big salaries and broken contracts, he had become one of the higher paid riders. To lure him from PDM, Panasonic had to pay at least $500,000 a year, a large raise.

Theunisse was having to spend some of that to defend himself. He reckoned his court and medical costs at more than $35,000, with no end in sight. It was worth it, he said, anything was worth it to clear his name and resume his career. That was why he went through continuing medical tests, riding his home trainer five and a half hours some days, losing up to 10 pounds, so that his urine samples could be tested before, during and after the ordeal. That was why he stopped every two hours during training rides and urinated into a flask.

"I keep telling myself that I'm crazy to ride with my jersey pockets stuffed full of urine samples. But I know I'm not crazy. I know I'm right."

His doctors were hoping to prove that the imbalance between his level of testosterone and epitestosterone was natural, not the result of steroids. Already a thick dossier reported that Theunisse's body produced three times as much testosterone as the average male and significantly less epitestosterone. Theunisse was waiting now to learn if the dossier would be accepted as proof by the International Cycling Union.

"I want to ride the Tour de France again," he said. "It's the best race in the world and my place is in it."

A Father's Fight

Yes, Jacques Sabatier acknowledged, his 13-year-old son Christophe had been found positive in a doping test. "This is the best thing that could have happened," he said with a pleased smile.

For years now, Sabatier has been fighting to clear the name of his older son, Cyril, who was found guilty of using steroids when he won the French junior cycling championship in June 1988, a month before his 17th birthday. He was believed to be the youngest French athlete ever to fail a drug test, but now that title has passed to Christophe, a cross-country runner and bicycle racer too.

"This proves what we have been saying," insisted Jacques Sabatier. "There is a medical abnormality that both boys share. And not just they. This is something not so rare among boys passing through puberty. It is for all boys everywhere, not just Cyril and Christophe, that we are fighting."

When he spoke at his home in Nimes, France, early in 1990, the battle showed signs of ending soon. After his long and unavailing campaign to persuade the French Cycling Federation, the Ministry for Youth and Sports and the International Olympic Committee to reinstate his son as France's junior champion, Sabatier took the case to court. He reported that the Council of State, France's highest legal authority, was near a binding ruling.

What if he did not win? "We'll lose, that's all." Did the thought discourage Sabatier? "Never," he said. "We'll win."

If the ruling was favorable, Sabatier said he would demand first the restoration of the title of junior champion to his son. "That's what this is all about," the father said, "clearing my son by restoring his title. After all these studies, it is clear that he takes no drugs. This is a point of honor."

"I want the jersey," said Cyril Sabatier as he sat in the family's living room in a housing project. He laughed at his choice of words since, pinned to the wall facing him, was that very blue, white and red jersey. "The title," Cyril Sabatier said, correcting himself. "Now it's Denis Marie who has it. Marie, who finished second."

Jacques Sabatier also plans to seek damages for bills that he estimates at more than 80,000 francs. That is a lot of money for the 38-year-old Sabatier, who nets less than 5,000 francs a month as a street sweeper in Nimes, and is far in debt. "I borrow," he said, "I keep borrowing." The money goes for legal advice, continuing medical tests for his son, trips between Nimes and the federation's offices in Paris and mammoth phone and postage bills.

A dossier that Sabatier has provided to officials and doctors in Europe and North America gives these details:

In the championships for riders aged 16 to 18 in June 1988, Cyril Sabatier easily won the first competition, a road race. He then provided a urine specimen which showed no trace of drugs when it was tested a week later. In the second day of competition, a time trial, Sabatier won again, provided a second urine specimen and went home with the gold medal and jersey.

More than a month later, on Aug. 6, the federation wrote the Sabatier family that a test of the second specimen had shown a level of testosterone, the natural male hormone, so far above what is regarded as normal that it was considered to be prima facie evidence of the use of anabolic steroids — synthetic and illegal derivatives of testosterone.

Precisely, Cyril Sabatier's level of testosterone to epitestosterone, a natural precursor of testosterone, was found to be eight to one. According to guidelines of the International Olympic Committee that have been in force for more than a decade, any ratio higher than six to one is proof of doping.

The Sabatiers have built their defense on the low level of epitestosterone produced first by Cyril and now by his brother. "The testosterone is not so high, but the epitestosterone is so low that the ratio is exaggerated," Jacques Sabatier said, producing a stack of medical reports. He speaks slowly and enunciates carefully, like a lawyer explaining a complicated case to a bewildered jury.

A basic exhibit in the dossier dates to July 1—7, 1989, when Cyril Sabatier was quarantined at the army base in Joinville, outside Paris, where the French military cycling team has its headquarters. Sharing a room with an official who kept him under constant supervision, the boy was allowed out only for training rides.

"Look," Jacques Sabatier exclaimed as his fingers darted up and down a page of figures. "Testosterone a little high, epitestosterone very low, ratio high. Testosterone a little high, epitestosterone very low, ratio high." The six days of surveillance showed the lowest ratio to have been just above the legal limit at 6.5, the highest 12.1. For the four other days the ratio was at least 9.

Sabatier produced another dossier, compiled after his younger son proved positive when he won a cross-country race. The hormonal levels and their ratio were similar to his brother's figures.

Both boys continue to compete and to do well. Cyril

Sabatier logs up to 600 kilometers a week in training with an amateur team in Provence allied with the professional Castorama team. "Cyrille Guimard has been watching Cyril since he was 15 years old," Jacques Sabatier said, referring to the Castorama manager who has guided three men to victory in the Tour de France.

On the closet door in his bedroom, which is full of bicycle wheels and some of the 70 trophies he has won, Cyril Sabatier has painted a picture of one of Guimard's winners, Bernard Hinault. Beneath it is written, "Barcelona 92," the site and date of the next Olympic Games. "The Olympics are my first priority," Cyril Sabatier said. "But, of course, I want to become a professional afterward. Everything I do is aimed at becoming a professional. Next month I'll ride in the amateurs' Paris–Roubaix, not with any hopes of winning, of course, but for the experience, for the chance to get a good result. Results are what attract professional managers."

He is the third generation in his family to race. His grandfather was good enough to compete in the 1950s in the Peace Race, the major East European race for amateurs, and Jacques Sabatier was a successful amateur until he quit at 19 to raise a family. He has been his son's coach and trainer since he started riding.

Of the three, Cyril Sabatier is by far the most promising. Before he won the junior championship, he was national champion for boys between 14 and 16 and has won six regional championships in the south of France. "I climb well, I've got endurance but I'm not very fast in the sprint," he judged. Despite the doping conviction, he was allowed to ride in the 1989 junior championships, where he did poorly, and was selected for the French team at the world championships in Moscow. Late in 1989 he set national records for three, five and 10 kilometers on a covered track and came back a week later to set national records at the same distances on an open track. He missed setting a world record for juniors by five seconds of the ride over 10 kilometers.

After both attempts, Cyril Sabatier tested negative for drugs, to his father's disappointment.

"We wanted to make the point that here was a champion, closely watched, and he still fails the tests the way they're given. We wanted to make that point before we went to court.

"He's absolutely clean," the father continued. "Here is his training diet: every day mashed potatoes, raw vegetables, fruit and a bit of red meat because an athlete needs it. His brother is a vegetarian. Everybody in the family, myself, my wife, the boys, eats only healthy food. We haven't opened a can of vegetables in this house in 10 years."

Sabatier was eager to keep showing dossiers, scrapbooks, even a cassette of a French television program that included a segment about his son's case. There, flickering on the screen, was Cyril Sabatier leaving the apartment to begin training ("Every day he walks up and down four flights of stairs with the bicycle on his shoulders," the father testified) and there he was himself, starting work at 4 AM to clean the streets of Nimes. Broom in hand, he stood in a cone of light for the television cameras while the city slept around him. "The good thing about this job is that I'm done by noon and I can spend the afternoons working to clear my son," he explained.

Jacques Sabatier waited until his boys were out of hearing before he summed up his long fight. "Listen," he said, "this is not only about making Cyril junior champion of France. This is also about making Cyril a man."

(In December 1990, the International Cycling Union ruled that Cyril Sabatier had proven his innocence and declared that his title as junior champion should be restored. The French Cycling Federation accepted this decision.)

Chapter 16
_____ Uphill Against the Clock

A day after he became the man to beat in the Tour de France, Ronan Pensec was beaten, and badly. Finishing far distant in an uphill time trial, he lost the yellow jersey in the 12th stage.

"Do I really have the yellow jersey?" gasped an unbelieving Claudio Chiappucci as he tried to recover his breath after crossing the finish line. Unofficially, the Italian knew he did. Chiappucci had been kept informed of his and Pensec's times by a Carrera team car during the 35.5-kilometer race against the clock from Fontaine, outside Grenoble, to the lushly green resort of Villard de Lans.

When Chiappucci asked the question Pensec was still out on the road and nothing was certifiable. Not until the Frenchman failed to cross the line 1 minutes 28 seconds after the Italian, did the jersey change hands. In fact, Pensec took nearly three minutes before he thrashed his way to the finish, now 1:17 behind and in second place. As he said later, people must have laughed to watch how slowly he negotiated the last two kilometers.

"I went well for the first five kilometers and that was it," Pensec continued. "After that, I felt as if I didn't have any

Short but nasty: The 33.5 km individual time trial from Fontaine to Villard-de-Lans is essentially all uphill.

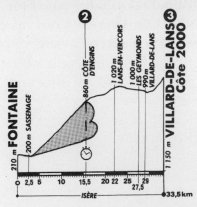

139

strength at all." He looked to the day off the next day to regain his power. "One minute 17 seconds, that's not so bad, is it? I've seen worse. And Chiappucci is alone. He doesn't have my team. And he's got the pressure on him now." Eyes downcast, Pensec sounded as if after his one day he fully understood what pressure the yellow jersey exerted.

The stage was won by the resurgent Erik Breukink in 56 minutes 52 seconds. Second, 30 seconds slower, was Pedro Delgado, who launched his drive to victory in the 1988 Tour with a victory in the same Villard de Lans time trial. Third, 43 seconds behind Breukink, was Miguel Indurain, who showed no signs of his collapse the previous day on Alpe d'Huez.

Efforts spent on that stage were prominent in Chiappucci's thinking about the yellow jersey. "I thought Pensec would be exhausted after his hard climb yesterday and so I went all out today," he said. Although he lost 38 seconds to Pensec at Alpe d'Huez, Chiappucci had remained confident, saying, "I feel strong and I haven't given up my dream of taking the yellow jersey." And now here it was.

Pensec was not the only one to show ill effects after the long climb. Greg LeMond, normally a fine time trialer and a marvel at recuperation, had to fight hard over the second half of the course to finish fifth overall, falling from third place to fourth behind Breukink.

LeMond, however, was really a big winner. With Pensec back in the Z jersey, the pale blue one with the puffy yellow cloud, the American was now free to work for himself and perhaps his second consecutive victory in the Tour. With half the race over, LeMond was finally unleashed. He was flourishing in the hot sun of the Alps and appeared ready to roll.

Breukink shared this evaluation. "I know Greg," he said, "and the only thing for him is winning. I look for Greg to attack in the Pyrenees."

Flight of the Eagle

The Eagle of Vizille flew over home soil. All along the way, past the dappled meadows and scarlet stands of poppies of the Vercors region, he was regarded with respect, as eagles usually are.

There was a time not so many years ago, however, when Thierry Claveyrolat carried the nickname in affectionate mockery. 'Eagle' is usually reserved for such great climbers as Federico Bahamontes, the Eagle of Toledo, who, legend says, once made it to the top of a mountain in the Pyrenees and was able to halt and eat an ice cream before the other riders joined him. Bahamontes won the king of the mountains jersey in six Tours de France. In 1959 he won the Tour itself and his yellow jersey still hangs in the rafters of the cathedral in Toledo.

Claveyrolat excelled in smaller races and smaller mountains for most of his career. Then, in 1989, he spread his wings. "For a while I thought I would become the world champion," he remembered. "I thought of it, I really thought it would happen."

His face puckered as he recalled the world championship course in Chambéry, France, and how he and eight others attacked on the eighth of 21 laps and built a lead of nearly five minutes. By the bell lap, Claveyrolat was one of three riders still ahead, by 11 seconds. At that point, his teammate Laurent Fignon led the pursuit, pulling with him Greg LeMond and Sean Kelly.

"It would have been better to believe in Claveyrolat," said another French rider, Charly Mottet.

Paced by Fignon, the threesome caught the leaders and LeMond went on to win the final sprint, with Claveyrolat fifth and Fignon sixth.

"If somebody had told me before the start, 'You'll be in front for 180 kilometers and finally finish fifth,' I would have been awfully happy," Claveyrolat admitted months later. "But because of the circumstances, I feel terrible. It would have been understandable if the Spaniards or the Italians had ridden after me, but not my own team.

"Winning would have been everything. For me it would have been more than a dream. But there's no point still thinking about it. I'll never forget the world championship at Chambéry but it's time now to think of other things."

Those other things included, of course, the Tour. Suddenly, at age 31, Claveyrolat bore the nickname of Eagle with pride. For the second successive year he was wearing the polka dot jersey of the king of the mountains in the Tour. In 1989 he lost the jersey when he had to quit in the Pyrenees because of a broken wrist, but now he was in sound health and even better form, winning the first Alpine stage and finishing fourth at Alpe d'Huez.

He explained that he had been inspired by his many fans in this part of the Alps near Grenoble. Claveyrolat comes from the town of Vizille, just outside city limits.

His supporters were back for the time trial from Fontaine, another suburb of Grenoble, to Villard de Lans. After his efforts the two previous days, the soft-spoken Claveyrolat did not expect to do well and seemed unsurprised when he finished 28th in the field of 170 remaining riders.

"I did my best," he said, "but I just didn't have anything left after the mountains." The fans who chanted his name along the route understood. "He's not a winner of the Tour de France, no," said Georges Delombre, who wore the cap of Claveyrolat's RMO team. "But he's a very good climber, he's won a stage of the Tour and he's one of us."

In the Vercors, Claveyrolat was 'the regional,' the local favorite, and in the countryside, where the Tour remains the favorite sport of summer, the tradition of cheering on the regional is strong.

In the village of Engins, for example, Maurice Francol had just led a herd of goats down from pasture and into a barn when the first rider in the time trial whirred past his farm. Francol barely turned to watch Antonio Espejo of the Kelme team take the curve. "I'm not much of a cycling fan," Francol confessed. "Farmers are too busy to spend the day watching even the Tour de France."

142

Would he be back by the road when Claveyrolat went by in the afternoon?

"Of course," he said. "He's one of us." Francol gestured at the craggy foothills of the Alps across from his barn. "He comes from the other side but still he's one of us."

Up the road a few hundred meters, near the banner that marked the summit of the Engins hill, Brigitte Durand was working at a snack stand. She is usually a secretary at the village hall but was helping sell sandwiches and such drinks as sodas, mineral water and beer.

"We're just here for the day, to make a little money and to cheer the riders," she explained. "Claveyrolat especially, of course. He's the regional."

At her side behind the wooden counter, Monique Dalbion nodded. "Claveyrolat especially, of course," she echoed.

Hours later, his back knotted and his jersey soaked with sweat as he climbed, the Eagle of Vizille came through Engins. The two women left their stand, which had sold out, and stood at the side of the road to join the chorus shouting, 'Thier-ry, Thier-ry.'

The rider swept left at the World War I monument. On the steps of the Restaurant du Barrage, a café really, a few farmers came out to join the cheering. Francol stood near his barn, where chickens scratched in the dirt, and applauded.

In a few seconds, Claveyrolat had left Engins behind as he rolled past the limestone hills overshadowing the road. He was on the descent now, with another long and tiring climb still to come. 'Vas-y, Thierry,' Go Thierry, the signs said as he approached the finish. He was weary by then and lost 2 minutes 49 seconds to the winner, Erik Breukink, falling from 15th to 16th place overall.

"That's done," Claveyrolat said. "I get my next chance in the Pyrenees." The Eagle of Vizille awaited another day to rise, to glide, to soar again.

Chapter 17

_____ A Day Off

The Tour settled into its one day off. Some riders, like Ronan Pensec, slept two or three hours later than usual, arising at 9:45 for breakfast. Others, like Greg LeMond, spent part of the day with their families. Some wives visited for the day, while LeMond's traveled most of the Tour with him, along with his parents.

The day was hot, even in the high atmosphere of the Vercors, and many riders spent time around a swimming pool. At some point, all riders went out for a few hours on their bicycles, just to keep the blood moving, just to keep their muscles toned, just because tradition said a rider should ride. Everybody connected with the race finds something to do, most often laundry, on a day off.

Some reporters went out to talk to the riders. They found a plucky Pensec, feeling good after 11 hours of sleep and willing to speak honestly.

"It was a total collapse," he admitted when he discussed the time trial. "Was it a _jour sans_?", the racers' term for that lost day, that long, empty feeling during a race that seems to strike many riders during a stage race. "Was it the pressure?" he continued. "I've lost the jersey, but I'm not the first to lose it in this Tour. Alcala collapsed, Pensec collapsed. Why not Chiappucci?

"But I'm not going to wait for him to collapse. There's only one thing to do and that's attack."

LeMond offered the same advice to Erik Breukink. Surrounded by journalists on the patio of his hotel once he returned from the day with his family in nearby Grenoble, LeMond was asked about the Dutchman. "If he wants to win the Tour, he's got to attack. It's not up to me to attack. What I hope is that Breukink isn't happy with his standing right now. If he likes third place and doesn't attack, he's never going to win this Tour."

144

The strongest rider, he continued, was Pedro Delgado. "I'm convinced that Delgado will put the pressure on."

If LeMond was thinking about Delgado, the Spaniard was thinking about Claudio Chiappucci. "He ought to be the third one to explode," Delgado judged. "One race should finish soon and the real one begin. But who knows? This is the Italians' year — Bugno, Argentin, why not Chiappucci too?"

Answering his own question, Delgado admitted that he suspected the final winner would be found among Breukink, LeMond and himself. "LeMond seems to be stronger than he was last year." So he liked LeMond's chances? Not really. "I worry more about Breukink," Delgado said. "What he did at Alpe d'Huez and in the time trial was pretty impressive. Plus he's ahead of me and LeMond."

For the record, Breukink asserted at his hotel that he was worried about LeMond and Delgado. Surrounded by his family at the same hotel, Raul Alcala said he liked Breukink's chances. "Sure, why not?" he asked.

Like Brahms toying with a theme from Haydn, reporters for the newspaper *l'Équipe* found a clever variation they could make their own: They interviewed the *directeurs sportifs* of all teams in the Tour and brought back their predictions of the final three-man victory podium in Paris. Counting three points for a prediction of victory, two points for a second place and one point for a third place, LeMond was the highest-ranked competitor with 37 points. Tied for second with 29 points were Delgado, Chiappucci and Breukink. Pensec was a distant fifth with five points, followed by Alcala with two points and Gianni Bugno with one point. Nobody else was given a chance.

LeMond impressed those coaches who knew him best, like Paul Koechli, now with Helvetia and formerly with La Vie Claire when LeMond rode for that team in 1985 and 1986. "The American never cracks," judged Koechli, giving his prediction of LeMond, Chiappucci and Delgado.

Similarly Maurice le Guilloux, now coach of Toshiba and formerly LeMond's teammate with La Vie Claire: "Greg is always strongest in the last week of the race, so...." His trio was LeMond, Delgado and Chiappucci.

Two other coaches who knew LeMond only long-range, Rafael Carrasco of Kelme and Cees Priem of TVM, also liked his chances. "The American, because the race is going to get tougher," said Carrasco. LeMond, because "He's the most relaxed of all the favorites," said Priem.

Delgado and Breukink picked up votes for the same reason — because the Pyrenees were only four days away. "Delgado will be unbeatable in the mountains," judged Bernard Vallet of RMO. "Delgado will have the home-field advantage in the Pyrenees," thought Jean-Luc Vandenbroucke of Lotto.

Jan Raas of Buckler liked Breukink. "The Pyrenees and the last time trial will make the difference," he said, leaving LeMond out of his trio of Breukink, Delgado and Chiappucci. Giancarlo Ferretti of Ariostea agreed. "Breukink will make up all the time needed in the Pyrenees and the last time trial."

Chiappucci had his supporters too. They included Jan Gisbers of PDM, who listed Chiappucci, Delgado and Le-Mond, saying of the Italian, "If he doesn't explode, he'll win." Willy Tierlinck of Histor-Sigma offered Chiappucci, Breukink and Delgado, reasoning "There's only one really hard stage left," and Peter Post of Panasonic liked Chiappucci, Breukink and LeMond, calling his favorite "a very good climber. The yellow jersey will give him wings." Bernard Quilfen of Castorama also liked Chiappucci ahead of Alcala and LeMond. "It's a *Tour à la Walkowiak*," Quilfen said.

A Tour à la Walkowiak? The French invoked that phrase every time an unknown seized the race's lead and threatened to make it stick. It rarely happened, of course, that a total outsider — so total that he never won a major race before or afterward — could steal off with victory in the world's greatest bicycle race. It hadn't happened, in fact, since 1956, when Roger Walkowiak did just that.

He was 29 years old and just another rider for the North-East-Center French team in the era when national and regional teams, instead of ones sponsored commercially, competed. His best results included second place in the 1953 Paris–Nice race and again second in the 1955 Dauphiné

Libéré, nowhere near good enough to qualify him for the French national team. Walko, as he was called, had a nice style on the bike, contemporaries remember, and he could climb passably, but he was too humble, too self-effacing to jump into the top rank.

For different reasons, most of the champions of the 1950s skipped the 1956 Tour: Jacques Anquetil was only 22 years old and concentrated that year on breaking the record for the hour's ride; Louison Bobet was recuperating from an operation; the magnificent Fausto Coppi and such lesser stars as Hugo Koblet, Ferdi Kubler, Jean Robic and Fiorenzo Magni had their own reasons to stay home. But Charly Gaul, the wonderful climber from Luxembourg, was there at the start in Rheims and so was was Federico Bahamontes, the equally wonderful climber from Spain. André Darrigade, who held the record for Tour stage victories that Eddy Merckx broke two decades later, was there and so was Stan Ockers, recently world champion on the road.

As fields go, it was a good one, and Walkowiak should have had no chance — except by a victory à la Walkowiak.

The decisive break came on the eighth stage, from Lorient into Angers, when 31 riders buried the pack 18 minutes behind. Walkowiak went into the yellow jersey and managed to hold it through the mountains to come and on into Paris. When the race ended, tens of thousands of fans whistled in disapproval and the overly humble Walko seemed to think the jeers were all aimed at him. He had not placed among the top three in any stage but still finished first by one minute 25 seconds over Gilbert Bauvin, another Frenchman.

The next year, resplendent for a day in the yellow jersey of the defending champion, Walkowiak joined the national team. Now, however, he was merely a teammate of Anquetil's, the *Wunderkind* who would win the Tour by nearly 15 minutes in his debut. Walkowiak abandoned early in the mountains.

He was back on the national team the next year, when Gaul was an easy winner and Walkowiak a distant 75th. The next Tour was Bahamontes's turn and Walkowiak was history. After his victory in 1956, the record books list only a third place in the 1958 Tour of the Southeast and a third place in the 1960 Circuit of the Auvergne.

The common explanation was that Walkowiak could not handle the pressure of having won the Tour de France. The whistles, they said, had shamed him terribly.

Not so, Walkowiak insisted as he startlingly paid his first visit to the Tour since 1967, when he was given its medal for meritorious service. He showed up briefly in the Alps, refused to explain why he was there instead of at home, shook the hands of some old-timers and offered a few brief interviews.

His old friend and teammate Raphael Geminiani once again tried to console him. Geminiani, a master at self-promotion, is still a part of the bicycle racing world, sometimes as high as a team coach, sometimes as low as a driver for a radio station. He learned how to build a reputation on a third-place finish in the 1958 Tour.

"Roger," said Geminiani the survivor, "you've got to get rid of this complex of Walkowiak, the fluke winner. I would have loved to win your Tour."

Walkowiak shook off Geminiani's embrace. "No," he said, "you've got it wrong. I've never had a complex. My problem is that I won the Tour just after Bobet and just before Anquetil. And that I never won anything else.

"My career was over quickly," he continued. "It wasn't a complex at all, but something I picked up in the Tour of Morocco, something intestinal." Old men are entitled to their beliefs.

Walkowiak had barely enough time for a few more remarks. "When I look at the race today and see the number of journalists, the cars that follow the riders, this huge party, I pinch myself and ask: Did I really win the Tour?" And then he was gone. Again.

Back to the Wars

Another outsider made the rounds on the Tour's day off. This

148

was Paul Kimmage, an Irishman who was shunned by the riders he had called his teammates only the year before.

He returned to competition at the 1990 Paris–Nice race, wearing a press pass, not a team jersey. After four years as a professional rider, Kimmage quit at the age of 27 and now writes for the *Sunday Tribune* in his hometown of Dublin. The newspaper also published his weekly column while he participated in his last competitive season. "I'm covering everything now, not simply cycling," he said. "Mainly I do interviews and human-interest stories."

Kimmage began as a journalist in 1988, when he covered the only Tour de France he did not compete in while he was a professional. "That work went down very well at home," he recalled. Nothing he has written, however, has had the impact of his first book, *A Rough Ride*. It details professional cyclists' use of banned drugs. "I'm explaining how we took them, what we took and why we did it," Kimmage said.

The prevalence of drugs, mainly steroids, is usually minimized by bicycle racing officials, even though the winner of the 1988 Tour de France, Pedro Delgado, and the winner of the 1983 and 1984 Tours, Laurent Fignon, have both tested positive in the last few years.

"We're labeled as cheaters for taking drugs," Kimmage continued, "but we're victims of a very bad system. That's the bottom line of the book."

Although he had not raced since the 13th stage of the 1989 Tour de France, and no longer had a professional license, Kimmage often says 'we' when he speaks about riders. He insisted, however, that he had no regrets about his decision to retire. "Maybe I'll miss it when the Tour comes around, but I don't think I will. I got out at the right time. I enjoyed the few years I had. I got the most out of myself. I could do no more. If I could have won the prologue in Paris–Nice, I'd say I wish I were back in it. But I know if I'd have ridden that prologue, I would have finished 84th or 85th."

He was being honest, not modest. "In my four years as a pro, I didn't exactly set the world alight," he noted. The record shows that his high points included finishing 131st in the

1986 Tour de France, 84th in the 1989 Giro d'Italia, 49th in the 1986 Liège–Bastogne–Liège classic, 8th in the 1986 Grand Prix of Plumelec and 8th in the 1987 Tour of Ireland. The closest he came to a victory was his ninth place one day in the 1986 Tour de France. "I had a stage win in front of me but I screwed up the sprint," he recalled. "I had the chance but I didn't take it."

Yet he had a fine career as an amateur racer, winning a handful of races in Ireland and continental Europe and finishing sixth in the 1985 world championship road race. That result led to a job with the RMO team in France for three years and then with the Fagor team in France for his final season.

"I lacked personal ambition as a professional," Kimmage said. "I was more happy to help the leader of the team than I was trying to do something for myself. I would give everything just for the leader of the team." He was a domestique, a servant — the rider sent ahead to chase a rival or sent back to the team car to fetch water bottles.

The leader Kimmage best served was his boyhood friend, Stephen Roche, who won the Tour de France, the Giro and the world championship in 1987. They shared a room during races. Kimmage was at Paris–Nice, in fact, to write a feature story about Roche for his Sunday paper. He came up with a fine one as Roche started a comeback from a serious knee injury by finishing second in the weeklong race. Whatever he wrote about Roche, Kimmage would never be indiscreet. "He tells me about things I could never write because they're so personal," he said. "He would perhaps come out the better if I did write them, but I can't break the confidence."

How then did Kimmage come to write a book, from the inside, about doping in bicycle racing? The answer is anger, a softspoken anger.

"There are one or two of my friends that have left cycling and have no job and have health problems. They've been badly treated by the whole system," Kimmage charged. "I have a nice job and no health problems and it would have been easy not to write the book. But it was thinking of these friends that made me say, 'Right, there have to be changes, this can't go on.'

"I don't think professional cycling comes out too good," he continued. "I have absolutely no apology to make for that — we're at fault. People are going to ruin this sport unless they wake up to the realities. I don't see why we should keep quiet about it."

The Irishman insisted that his motive was not to settle scores. "I don't name names as far as possible. Insofar as putting the finger on bigger riders, I don't do any of that. I wrote what I saw, not what I heard. In that way it's totally honest.

"We're talking about the lack of controls in races," he said, referring to drug tests. "This is big business. These races give points, and riders earn their salaries on the basis of those points. So the temptation to take the stuff to earn more points is enormous. If there are no controls, you can't expect fellows not to succumb to the temptation. Ultimately we're not to blame."

He was still saying 'we.'

The Chain Gang of the Road

Drugs and bicycle racing go way back together, as far as the last century. The sport's first death suspected to have been caused by drugs dates to 1896 and the fifth Bordeaux–Paris race, which was won by Arthur Linton, a former miner in Wales. Two months later he was dead and the cause was thought to be an overdose of cocaine, then a not-uncommon restorative for riders.

Three decades later, during the 1924 Tour, the French journalist Albert Londres wrote a celebrated article about Henri and Francis Pélissier, brothers who had just quit the race in Cherbourg. Londres titled the article "The Chain Gang of the Road."

" 'You have no idea what the Tour de France is all about,' Henri said, 'it's a Calvary... How we suffer on the road. But do you want to see how we make it? Look.'

"From his bag, he took a phial.

" 'This is cocaine for the eyes and that's chloroform for the gums.... And pills? Do you want to see pills?'

"They each showed three boxes.

" 'In short,' Francis said, 'we ride on dynamite.' "

The sport continued to ride on dynamite, insisting that the use of stimulants under medical supervision was beneficial to the racers, until 1966, when the Tour began drug tests under a new French law banning doping by athletes. After the first test, the riders staged a protest strike, slowing down and then walking with their bicycles for a few minutes before resuming the stage to Bayonne.

The next Tour was marked by a death. Tom Simpson, the popular Englishman who won the world championship in 1965, fell three kilometers from the summit of the desolate and blazingly hot Mont Ventoux in Provence. Helped back onto his bicycle, he rode another kilometer before he collapsed again. Unconscious, Simpson was taken by a helicopter to Avignon, where he was pronounced dead early in the evening. Phials marked with the trade name of an amphetamine were found in his jersey and others were found in his baggage.

The official medical report said Simpson, then 29, had died of heart failure brought on by exhaustion. "Unfavorable weather conditions, intense overexertion and the use of dangerous medicine could have contributed to the exhaustion." Experts confirmed that traces of stimulants were found in his blood, urine, stomach and intestines.

His death was much mourned and a memorial was built at the spot on Mont Ventoux where he fell. Nevertheless, Jacques Anquetil, who had already won five Tours de France, challenged the new testing rules again that fall when he broke the record for the hour's ride on the track in Milan. For refusing to provide a urine specimen immediately, as International Cycling Union regulations now specified, Anquetil was penalized by not having his record recognized.

It was broken, anyway, a month later. And, as Paul

Kimmage knows, drugs continue to be used. "To dope the racer is as criminal, as sacrilegious, as trying to imitate God: it is stealing from God the privilege of the spark," judged Roland Barthes, the French *savant* and Tour de France fan.

Chapter 18
_____ Transition Stage

The 13th stage, from Villard de Lans to St. Étienne, a short and rolling 149 kilometers, was expected to fit into the framework of transition days — stages between one major rendezvous, in this case the Alps, and another, the Pyrenees. By tradition, transition days are left to secondary riders to fight it out for the stage victory that satisfies their honor and their sponsors' desire for publicity. Nobody declares a truce, though, and leaders are free to attack.

Attacking was exactly what Greg LeMond had in mind, and his Z team with him. "We decided to toughen the race," revealed Roger Legeay, the Z coach. "We didn't know what to think about Chiappucci and we decided to find out. The easiest way was to toughen the race and see if we couldn't get him to self-destruct by pushing his team to the limit."

The strategy worked brilliantly. From the start, when Phil Anderson of TVM — just the sort of rider, low in general classification but high in ambition, who looks for a victory on a transition day — attacked on the steep descent from Villard de Lans to the blazing plains of the Rhône Valley, the pack was forced to work hard. It covered the first 34 kilometers in 38 minutes. The French especially were riding, seeking a victory on this Bastille Day.

Two more breaks were undone, with the Carrera team riding all-out to protect its leader. At kilometer 55, the fourth attack developed, and this time Ronan Pensec went off with a group of 30 riders on a short, steep hill. They soon had a lead of 1:36 on Chiappucci, more than wiping out Pensec's deficit of 1:17. The attack was too serious to be left unanswered.

Surprisingly, Chiappucci led his Carrera teammates in pursuit and they whittled the lead group down to six riders by kilometer 105. The work was hot, tiring and close to fatal for Chiappucci, who admitted later that he should have left the chasing to his teammates. He had nothing left to give when LeMond suddenly attacked, taking with him Erik Breukink. "I saw that Carrera and especially Chiappucci were shot, so I decided to go," LeMond said. "I was worried that Breukink would refuse, but he agreed and we went." Joined by Miguel Indurain of Banesto, Andy Hampsten of 7-Eleven, Eduardo Chozas of ONCE and Roberto Conti of Ariostea, they swept past the six leaders and began the second breakaway to blow open the Tour.

If Chiappucci was unable to follow, Pedro Delgado still felt strong but, unfortunately for him, had decided to shadow the Italian. By the time he realized that he had missed the big break, its lead was 1:30. Delgado counterattacked 10 kilometers later at the start of a 10-kilometer climb to the Croix de Chaubouret pass. He cut the lead to 75 seconds before Indurain was ordered to drop back and tug him along, which he did strongly enough to reduce the lead to 20 seconds at the 1,201-meter summit.

Down the descent LeMond drove his group of five and into St. Étienne, where he waved the others ahead to fight out the sprint. In a contest without a true sprinter, Chozas managed to get his wheel across the line first. "The sprint?" LeMond asked. "It didn't interest me at all." He would have been the logical winner but feared that his presence would have caused enough slowdowns and maneuverings to cost the group 30 seconds.

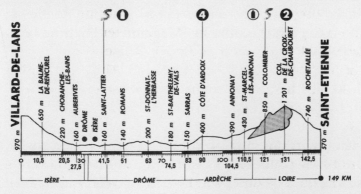

The 13th stage from Villard-de-Lans to Saint-Etienne.

That was exactly the time behind that Delgado, Marino Lejarreta and Gianni Bugno finished. Struggling far back, Chiappucci lost 4:53. The lead that seemed so vast only the day before was now barely above two minutes. LeMond had taken a serious option on another victory in the Tour de France.

For once, Chiappucci had something to say. He had been so overwhelmed by what had happened to put him into the yellow jersey two days before, even Italian reporters had failed to extract anything useful from an interview with him. As a loser, Chiappucci turned articulate. "I made a mistake," he admitted. "I never should have done all that work chasing Pensec. I should have waited for things to develop." He looked around beseechingly. After years of success with such formidable leaders as Stephen Roche and Roberto Visentini, the Carrera team was weak and had entered the Tour only out of force of habit. As Chiappucci knew, he was the sort of rider who was accustomed to working for a leader, not being one. Of course he had pitched in when things got rough: That was his training and, until this race, his job.

So there was nothing small-minded about it when he pointed out that at least he had the satisfaction of seeing Pensec caught. He had finished nearly three minutes behind Chiappucci and was now effectively removed as a potential Tour winner.

That was the sort of pleasure Chiappucci was accustomed to taking when he rode for his leader. The man in the yellow jersey just didn't get it; he seemed to be expecting Roche or Visentini to come along, ruffle his hair and tell him he had done just fine.

On the Roller Coaster

Stephen Roche wasn't ruffling any teammate's hair these days and thanking him for his support. The Irishman, ordinarily so affable, was outspokenly critical of his new teammates with Histor-Sigma and with some of his former ones with Fagor.

In a wide-ranging interview with *l'Équipe*, Roche ducked charges by Robert Millar, now of Z, that he had abandoned 18 teammates by quitting Fagor so late during the winter that it had no alternative except to drop out of the sport. Not so, said Roche. "I think Millar doesn't have the heart for this sport and I'm the first to say how sorry I am for him because I like him a lot," the Irishman retorted.

Another former teammate, Paul Kimmage, was also a source of despair. Kimmage's book had appeared and earned him a chorus of criticism, mainly from riders who admitted they had not read it. Roche had, he underlined, and didn't like some of the secrets it spilled.

There was, for example, Kimmage's account of how Roche had bought a criterium in Dublin. It wasn't good for the sport to reveal such things, Roche said, conveniently forgetting that he told the story first in a book of his own. Then there was the Irish television program where Kimmage had been asked whether Roche and Sean Kelly had ever taken drugs during a major race. Kimmage had refused to answer, saying that he stood by his book, which never said that either Irish champion used drugs. "His silence provoked a lot of trouble, a big question mark," Roche charged. "It seemed simpler to me to say that we're always checked during a race."

He was in a bad mood, no doubt about it, and his lack of results had much to do with his feelings: Far back in every climb and time trial, Roche did not rank among the first two dozen in this Tour. And so continued his long and heady free-fall from 1987, when a quarter of a million Dubliners turned out to cheer him the day after he became the first Irishman to win the Tour de France. A month later he won the world championship road race as well, joining only Eddy Merckx in finishing first in the Giro d'Italia, the Tour and the Worlds in the same year. For that feat, he was named Ireland's man of the year.

In Dublin they delighted in retelling the story of the milkman's boy who credited his start in cycling with keeping him out of trouble by diverting him from a rough crowd. The newspapers were full of the apocryphal tale of how he saved for months to buy a cheap bicycle that he assembled the night before the 1975 Irish junior national championships, and then finished third.

True or false, this was the stuff of legend: how Roche took a leave of absence as a maintenance fitter at a dairy and went to the Continent as an amateur racer, hoping to make his name and turn professional, and how his leave was ending in 1980 and he still had not attracted a professional sponsor.

"What do I have to do?" he asked his coach at the ACBB club just outside Paris.

"What have you done? Win a big race." So he finished first in the demanding Paris–Roubaix race and then again in Paris–Rheims and was signed by Peugeot.

He broke in spectacularly in 1981, winning four big races, and then failed to win again until 1983. In 1985 he was third in the Tour de France and in 1986 again failed to win a race. That winter he tore up his left knee in a fall at the Paris Six-Day race and was bothered by knee problems for years afterward.

Still that did not keep him from sweeping the three major races of 1987. Roche was not quite 28 years old then and seemed able to dominate bicycle racing for seasons to come. He didn't, though, and has barely recorded a major victory since his golden year.

It is a cautionary tale. Personable and witty though he is, Roche was planning to join his fourth team in five years, the new Tonton Tapis team in Belgium. His career has often been marked with feuds, recriminations, accusations of betrayal and even, briefly, a revolt against a sponsor in which Roche led most of his Fagor team in a weeklong walkout. In Ireland he is said to have lost some of his magic popularity of 1987 because of his lack of results over the last three years. His repeated explanations of how his knee injury has hampered him have left some people wondering if he has not simply found a convenient excuse. The word out is that Roche may have become a complainer.

When he moved from the disbanded Fagor team in France

to Histor-Sigma in Belgium in 1990, he was full of praise for his new teammates, but spent most of the rest of the year being bitterly critical of them. "All they wanted was to be the best Belgian team," he charged. "Their world didn't stretch beyond that. "During the week they rode all the *kermesses*," the exhibition races that are a specialty in Belgium, "and on the weekend, when the real racing comes, they were tired."

So was he, Roche admitted after the Tour. He reported that he was advised by his doctor that he had an insufficiency of minerals and vitamins — "I'm very low in zinc, iron, potassium, you name it" — and badly needed a rest. Another season without results was behind him.

Roche understandably prefers not to discuss the past. "I'm reasonably happy, I'm coming back to my old self and now I know why I've had these problems," he said. "I knew it wasn't normal. For too long it's like I've been riding against wheels with 28 spokes while I've only had ten. Even with ten spokes, the wheel still goes around, but not without difficulty."

Chapter 19

_____ Outsider's Day

Claudio Chiappucci had learned something the day before and, solid professional that he was, applied the lesson. On the 205-kilometer 14th stage from Le Puy en Velay to Millau, Chiappucci was again left behind, but this time continued to ride at his own pace. "Z and Banesto tried everything to get me to explode again, but this time I rode differently," he said proudly. "I saved myself for the last climb and I had enough left to handle it." Finishing 13th, 47 seconds down, he still lost 13 more seconds to Greg LeMond, Pedro Delgado and Erik Breukink.

"Those are the ones who'll fight it out for the final victory," the Italian predicted. "I can't tell who's strongest." Then he brightened. "But I'm still first, aren't I? Every extra day in the yellow jersey is an extra day of glory."

The stage was won by Marino Lejarreta, who was riding in his third major tour of the year, as he did most seasons. Nearing age 33, Lejarreta had now ridden in 10 Vueltas, 6 Giros and 7 Tours de France. He had finished as high in the Tour as fifth in 1989 but never before won a stage.

"I didn't think it would happen this year, because the race has been so fast," he said. On the rest day, his coach, Manuel Saiz, took the Basque aside and spoke to him encouragingly for two hours. It wasn't enough simply to be present, Saiz told him, the object was to win.

So, two kilometers from the finish on a steep first-category climb, Lejarreta attacked. All the leaders were just behind him but he held them off, pushing Miguel Indurain into second place by 24 seconds.

The pack looked weary as it struggled in, broken into small groups as much as 38 minutes behind. Four riders, including notably Flavio Giupponi, the nominal leader of Chiappucci's Carrera team, had abandoned on a sweltering day replete with attacks. "There were so many attacks that I wasn't sure

160

66. Above: His jersey unzipped in the heat, Greg LeMond stays with Pedro Delgado but refuses to relay him up Alpe d'Huez. (photo Presse-Sports)

67. Below: Robert Millar cools himself off on the climb as he paces teammate Ronan Pensec. (photo Presse-Sports)

69. Above right: Officials help Olaf Ludwig who struggled in far behind. (photo Presse-Sports)

68. Above left: Gianni Bugno nips LeMond for the stage victory. (photo Cor Vos)

70. Below: Claudio Chiappucci beams after gaining the yellow jersey on the 12th stage. (photo Presse-Sports)

71. Above: Erik Breukink seems determined at the time trial — which he won easily. (photo Presse-Sports)

72. Right: The Irish former Tour racer Paul Kimmage, wearing a press pass now. (photo Presse-Sports).

73. Left: Andy Hampsten, wet but happy. (photo Presse-Sports)

74. Below: LeMond leads the five-man breakaway on the 13th stage that helped him regain nearly five minutes. (photo Presse-Sports)

75. Above: Frequent attacks characterize a transition day from the Alps on the way to the Pyrenees. (photo Presse-Sports)

76. Below: And sometimes the breakaways manage to build a fair-sized lead. (photo Presse-Sports)

77. Left: Before the stage start, some of the Tour's motorcycle escorts are off socializing. (photo Presse-Sports)

78. Below: Despite the armada of policemen, once in a while an ordinary *cyclotouriste* manages to join the Tour. (photo Presse-Sports)

79. Right: Sean Kelly, hoping for a stage victory. (photo Presse-Sports)

80. Below: As Spanish fans wave the Basque flag to cheer on Miguel Indurain and Marino Lejarreta, the Tour climbs to Luz Ardiden on the 16th Stage. (photo Presse-Sports)

81. Left: At the finish on Luz Ardiden, Indurain looks back to check how far LeMond trails him. (photo Presse-Sports)

82. Not long before, on the way up, LeMond was the one to look back and see both Basques are right with him — Indurain, center, and Lejarreta, left. (photo Presse-Sports)

83. Right: The pack leaves the grotto at Lourdes and heads for Pau on the 17th stage. (photo Presse-Sports)

84. Below: Pedro Delgado, right, and Claudio Chiappucci attack on the Marie Blanque climb in the Pyrennees. (photo Presse-Sports)

85. Above: Greg
LeMond frets after a
flat left him
vulnerable on the
17th stage. (photo
Cor Vos)

86. Left: His wheel
replaced, LeMond
sets off again on the
Marie Blanque.
(photo
Presse-Sports)

87. Above: From behind, the Z team helps bring LeMond back to the leaders. (photo Presse-Sports)

88. Below: From ahead, LeMond leads Z on the descent. (photo Presse-Sports)

89. Above: Fetching water on a hot day: Peter de Clerq of Lotto.
(photo Presse-Sports)

90. Below: Yes, it was very hot, and Sean Yates of 7-Eleven
welcomes a good hosing down. (photo Presse-Sports)

91. Above: Thierry Marie of Castorama hams it up on the 19th
stage by wearing a beret he snatched from a spectator's head.
(photo Cor Vos)

92. Below: In the 20th stage time trial, LeMond disdained disk
wheels and a plunging frame but used triathlete bars. (photo Presse-
Sports)

93. Above: Claudio Chiappucci starts the decisive time trial without any aerodynamic aid. (photo Presse-Sports)

94. Left: As the Eiffel Tower attests, the Tour approaches the Champs-Élysées on the 21st stage. (photo Presse-Sports)

95. Above: Victor and vanquished. Now in the yellow jersey, Le-
Mond exchanges salutes with Chiappucci on the final stage. (photo
Presse-Sports)

96. Turning left at the Joan of Arc statue into the Rue de Rivoli, the
riders head for the finish of the 77th Tour de France. (photo Presse-
Sports)

97. Above: Johan Museeuw easily wins the final sprint. (photo Cor Vos)

98. Below: Greg LeMond accepts the bowl that goes to the winner of the Tour de France. (photo Presse-Sport)

there was nobody ahead of me when I crossed the line," Lejarreta confessed. "I wasn't sure whether to lift my arms or not."

He finished half an hour ahead of the fastest time predicted by the race's organizers. And this was the day after the St. Étienne stage had been raced at a near-record speed of 44.65 kilometers an hour. Whatever happened to uneventful transition days?

Just Say No

Andy Hampsten, "the other American," was having a pretty good Tour too. Ranked 10th overall and a strong climber, he was looking forward with newfound confidence to the Pyrenees. "It was fun being in front again," he said of the five-man breakaway into St. Étienne.

Yes, Greg LeMond, long identified as 'the American,' was now in excellent position to win his second successive Tour. And yes, Hampsten was hoping, at best, to finish among the top five and perhaps win a mountain stage. But don't think Hampsten was bothered by being referred to as "the other American," as French newspapers often called him.

"It flatters me," he said. "I get a big kick from going from a kid riding his bike around North Dakota to being ranked with somebody at the top of his favorite sport. Put that way, it kind of tickles me."

Hampsten was displaying a fair amount of confidence, which he admits he has not always had. "If I can put it all together, nobody can beat me," he said before the Tour began. "But I don't always believe I can put it all together. A lot of it is confidence, so that I don't defeat myself."

Often accused of being the thinking man's bicycle racer — always reading a serious book or visiting an art gallery or cathedral between stages — Hampsten felt he had thought too hard, too long about his confidence.

So had he stopped overthinking?

"No," he replied with a laugh. "I do that more than ever.

It's like so many things in life: Just because you know it's not good for you, you can't always stop doing it."

In addition to confidence, Hampsten had worked long and hard at "things I'm not so good at," as he put it. These included mainly time trialing, where his consistently so-so results guaranteed that he could not win the Tour. He could submerge this weakness in other major stage races, as he did in winning the Giro in 1988, but the Tour was simply too oriented toward time trials to allow him much hope.

That was a shame because the race meant so much to him. "The Tour de France, for me, is everything," he admitted. "Everything" included a platform for Hampsten to speak.

He would like to win the Tour some day for most of the usual reasons, including fame and fortune, and for a special purpose as well: to speak out against the use of drugs in a sport bedeviled by them.

"If I do win, it would be a good example for me to say, 'Anyone can do it without drugs,' " he said. He is particularly concerned for the image that professional bicycle racing presents to youth. "Young people who want to get into the sport, they hear, or have the idea, that it's full of drugs and they lose interest," Hampsten continued. "Or they think they have to use drugs to do it and when they're very young, they're already damaging their bodies."

Hampsten is outspoken in his condemnation of drugs, mainly steroids and stimulants. "Bike racing is a hard sport," he said. "The reason it fascinates people is because it's a brutally hard sport. It's supposed to be hard. So if you're just taking pills to take the pain away, it's not much of a sport, is it?"

He is especially critical of the medical inspection program in the Tour. "When we do our medical tests at the start, they should look for everything," he said. "Now there are no urine samples, no drug testing. Tell people a year in advance that you're going to test for drugs and, if they fail, they're out of the race."

Still, he had some good words for the daily drug tests given to the winner of each stage, two riders selected at random and the overall leader at the start of the stage. "I think cycling was the first sport to have drug testing," he said. "We're doing something about it. I'm disgusted that in my sport there is a drug problem, but at least we're confronting it."

Confining his comments to interviews and public statements, Hampsten said he was not part of any organization that opposes drugs. "I'm not a politician," he insisted when asked if he was planning a broader campaign. "I simply don't think drugs have any place in the sport. Obviously they change the sport. They change the lives of people who use them and they make it harder for people who don't use them to keep up.

"I think people ride better without drugs than with drugs. That's a different attitude than some European riders have, different from the tradition at least.

"So, yes," Hampsten said of the prospects of his victory. "I think it would show young riders, especially, that in the long run drugs are not going to help you."

Hampsten was in the forefront of those few rider who condemned Pedro Delgado in 1988 when the Spaniard tested positive for using probenecid, a masking drug for steroids. The Delgado case was the most publicized of three positive findings — including that of Gert-Jan Theunisse — among the 198 riders in the '88 Tour. The year before two riders were found positive; none have been since '89, when testing procedures were somewhat tightened.

"I can't say other riders use drugs," Hampsten continued. "Some do, obviously, since they're caught doing it. But I don't know if it's just them or if 90 percent of the pack uses them." Most general estimates put the use of steroids and stimulants much lower than that. But in France alone, more than 30 riders at all levels tested positive in 1987, the last year such figures were made public.

Part of the reason, as Hampsten indicated, is the overall attitude of European riders to drug use. A typical remark came from Teun Van Vliet, formerly a talented rider for Panasonic and now, before his 30th birthday, retired after a stomach operation. Van Vliet said he had never tested positive for drugs.

Asked about the Delgado drug scandal, Van Vliet corrected his questioner: "I'm sorry, but it wasn't a drug scandal because it wasn't on the list. So there was no drug result. He was really negative, not positive."

What if an opponent did test positive for a banned drug? Here Van Vliet drew a common distinction.

"It depends on what kind of medicine he used," he said, avoiding the use of the word 'drugs.' He added that sometimes riders needed medicine because they were ill.

"It's your profession, so you have to do it," he pointed out. "Somebody who's working in an office and who's ill, he sees the doctor and the doctor says, 'I'll give you something, but you can't go to the office because you're positive.' That's crazy."

He was not speaking with Hampsten, but the American had already offered a response: "I think I'm a fairly talented rider who can go pretty far without drugs. Some people might argue that if I used drugs, I could ride better."

How would he answer them?

"I don't have to," Hampsten insisted. "To me it doesn't mean a thing. If someone tells me, 'You would have won this race if you'd taken these pills,' it's not even within my realm of options.

"It's like saying, 'If you wiggle your ears and wish, you'll be on top of this mountain.' " He laughed at the thought of climbing the Alps that way.

Chapter 20
___ Day of the Unsung Heroes

Finally, an old-fashioned transition day, with heroics by such riders as Charly Mottet, 37th and more than 31 minutes behind when the 170-kilometer 15th stage from Millau to Revel began. Or the unsung Giuseppe Calcaterra of Chateau d'Ax, 116th and 1:18:33 down, Slava Ekimov of Panasonic, 74th and 1:1:07, and Edwig Van Hooydonck of Buckler, 109th and 1:15:17.

Mottet's victory was so meaningless that even *l'Équipe*, usually the most chauvinist of newspapers, refused to be carried away to frog heaven. The French in general were riding badly, with Fabrice Philipot of Castorama the highest ranked at 14th overall. Laurent Fignon hadn't made it out of Normandy and Jean-François Bernard, at 28 a somewhat aging young hope, was last heard from before the Alps, where he predictably quit. In short, it was another Tour without *de France*.

Mottet was a perennial bust in the Tour, and even when he finished second to Gianni Bugno in the Giro, it was difficult to believe that this was the year he would finally fulfill what was still thought of as his potential. A star time trialer in the Grand Prix des Nations, he came up empty in every race

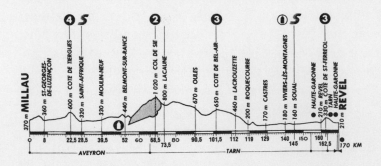

The 20th stage from Millau to Revel.

against the clock in the Tour. A smashing climber in the Dauphiné Libéré, he sank without trace on many of the same mountains in the Tour.

For years he had broken hearts at *l'Équipe*, which traditionally listed him among the favorites. On the computer, he had ranked as high as first among the world's top 600 professionals, but when it came to the big race, the pressure was too great for Mottet.

Only a week before, he had confessed that now, approaching his 28th birthday, he didn't want to fool himself. Perhaps it was time to say that he was not ever going to win the Tour. Perhaps it was time, he continued, to start thinking of stage victories instead. This was his first.

"The New Mottet Arrives," said the headline deep inside *l'Équipe*. Of Calcaterra, Ekimov and Van Hooydonck, there was barely a word. It was that kind of stage.

The Man who was King

This was not the long-awaited day for Sean Kelly, the man who was and would again be king, even if just for a day, if that day occurred in the Tour de France.

Discussing his hopes of a stage victory, Kelly was blunt. "This year I have more of a chance because I'm a long way down in the general classification," he said. He was in 23d place, 23:24 behind Claudio Chiappucci, and worrying — although he hesitated to admit it — about his continuing inability to win a stage in the Tour. For a rider who ranked for years at the top of the computerized standings and who still had not dropped out of the first dozen, he had not stood on the Tour's daily victory podium for a long while.

"Yes," he said flatly, "it's been a few years now since I won a stage." To be precise, he recorded the last of his five stage victories in 1982.

Now, in the final few years of his career, Kelly was running out of time. "A lot of people say this is my last Tour," he noted. "But I haven't said it. I haven't decided at all. I don't think

166

age matters when you still have good results and perform well."

That he was doing. Recovering from a collarbone broken in the Tour of Flanders in March, he had returned in June to win the Tour of Switzerland. In the Tour, he had worked long and hard for his PDM teammates. Was that really Kelly who fetched water bottles on the climb to Alpe d'Huez? Had King Kelly, now nearing his 35th birthday, become a domestique? The answers were yes and, of course, no. Kelly did indeed go to the team car for bidons on the climb, but he fixes with a cold stare anybody who dares suggest he does that for a living.

"You can't really say I was fetching bidons. It was in the hard mountains and the other guys weren't there," he explained, referring to the team's usual domestiques. Only Kelly, Uwe Ampler, and PDM's co-leaders, Erik Breukink and Raul Alcala, were at the front. "I decided that somebody had to fetch the bidons and I decided to do it quickly. It was the only time I fetched the bidons in this race."

Had he considered ordering one of the others — perhaps Ampler, the first-year professional from East Germany — to get the water? "It was a very difficult moment in the race, everybody storming a bit, and you don't start talking to others then. You don't start talking about getting bidons, you just do it and that's it."

That's Kelly's Law: You just do it. A corollary is that you don't agonize over it afterward, no matter what the 'it' is. Not even if it was his lack of success at winning a stage. After briefly making a run at the Charly Mottet breakaway, Kelly had subsided, finishing 4:48 behind, in 24th place for the stage.

There was a time, although he did not mention it, when he never could have based his hopes on the fact that he was no threat. King Kelly he was called in the mid-1980s, when he dominated the sport, sweeping the classics and riding strongly in most stage races, winning Paris–Nice an astonishing seven straight times, winning the Vuelta de España in 1988, finishing as high as fourth in the Tour de France in 1985.

He was a feared sprinter then, one of the toughest and fastest in the pack. Now, he admits, he no longer has his sprint. "Last year was the same situation," he said. "I'm not as fast as I was and there are some very good sprinters who've come along the past two or three years." He brushed off a suggestion that age had caught up to him. "First of all," he said, "if you don't work at something, you lose it, and definitely the sprint is something I don't work at. Secondly, if you ride in the mountains always at the front, it takes effect on your sprint. The sprinters always stay behind and take it easy in the mountain stages and then, on the flat stages, they're there.

"You have to take those things into account," he concluded, without a trace of asking for pity.

Pity has never been Kelly's way. A farm boy and former bricklayer at home, he came to France as a teenage amateur rider and then served a long and anonymous apprenticeship as a leadout rider for Freddy Maertens and Michel Pollentier, Belgian stars of the 1970s. Known for his dedication and work ethic, Kelly acknowledges that the 170 races a year he used to ride — 30 or 40 more than most other professionals — took their toll each summer in the Tour.

"In my good years, maybe I made too many races, making 170 races a year, which is by far too much," he said. "With a lighter load then, I might have had better results in bigger races like the Tour de France."

He acknowledged that not many others are cast in his mold. "Some riders coming up now are not really interested in working," he said, refusing, as usual, to name names. Although he is known to be critical of the training methods of some of the Eastern Europeans coming into the sport, Kelly has always been careful not to embarrass either teammates or rivals. "That's certain individuals," he added, "but in general I don't think it's changed too much.

"The style of racing has changed in the last six, seven years. You go back then and a team had one leader and everybody worked for him. Now a team has three, four or five guys capable of winning a race, maybe not so much in the

168

Tour but in smaller races and classics. That's because of multinational sponsors — they want the publicity of winning, so you have to have three, four guys capable of winning.

"And the money has gotten so much better over the years. But in relation to other sports we're still so much behind except for some contracts." One of the better ones is his own, which was reported to be worth $750,000 a year when he first signed with PDM late in 1988.

He probably remained near that level when he renewed the contract in 1990. It runs for two years, after which Kelly expects to return fulltime to Ireland. "Another two years will see me finished," he said. One big reason was his new status as a father after the birth of twins, Nigel and Stacey. "I don't see the twins very much," he said. "Under two years of age it's not so bad, but when they get older — two, three years of age — when you go away they miss you more."

When he leaves, he will go with no regrets, he insisted. "I was brought up on a farm, served my time as a bricklayer and, if I hadn't become a rider, I'd probably still be a bricklayer. In bike racing, I've done very well at it, I've made a name for myself, I've made a lot of money and I don't regret anything at all."

Chapter 21
___ Long Trek in the Pyrenees

With a magnificent ride over three major peaks in the Pyrenees, Greg LeMond moved into second place overall, closed to five seconds behind the leader, appeared to burn off all other rivals and position himself for his second successive victory in the Tour.

Despite the great day in his life, the American had few of the pure fruits of victory. He finished the 215-kilometer stage from Blagnac to the mountaintop resort of Luz Ardiden in second place and was unable to take the yellow jersey from Claudio Chiappucci, who finished 2 minutes 19 seconds behind LeMond. But there was no mistaking the American's joy as he hugged his wife Kathy and a longtime friend and adviser, Fred Mengoni, at the finish line after the 16th stage.

An ecstatic LeMond refused to say that the race was all but over. "I hope so," he said, "but it's not won until we finish on the Champs-Élysées." Or it's not over until it's over.

Told that he had gained 1:32 on the rider he considered his most dangerous rival, Pedro Delgado, who had finished eighth, LeMond burst into a big grin and said redundantly, "I'm very happy about that." He gained even more time on

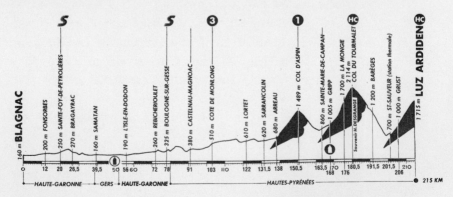

The 21st stage from Blagnac to Luz Ardiden is long and hard, with some of the Tour's toughest climbs.

Erik Breukink, who finally succumbed to the *jour sans* — the empty day — that has marked each of his Tours de France. Finishing 4:16 behind LeMond, Breukink fell from second to fourth place in general classification as Delgado moved up to third.

The stage, raced under sometimes cloudy skies in heavy heat, was watched by hundreds of thousands of fans. Many of them were Spaniards from just across the Pyrenees and many of those were Basques. Flapping their yellow and red flags, they were rewarded with a victory by Miguel Indurain, Delgado's lieutenant with Banesto. After staying on LeMond's rear wheel for the last seven kilometers, Indurain jumped off with 500 meters to go and cruised in first by six seconds. If the victory, after LeMond had entirely set the pace, seemed unfair to some of the non-Spanish spectators, LeMond accepted it as part of the sport. He was still looking for his first stage victory but had other things to celebrate.

For one, there was the narrowing of his deficit with Chiappucci, who rode a gallant race and even jumped off to an unexpected attack at the start of the first climb, following Jorg Mueller of TVM. "I didn't intend to attack," Chiappucci said. "I was simply riding at the front and went with Mueller when he attacked. I looked back and saw that we had opened a gap. That's when I decided to go all out. I thought the others would hesitate and it was worth taking a chance."

As his rivals seemed to wait for each other to react first, Chiappucci was first by 45 seconds over the Aspin peak, 1,489 meters high and rated first category in height and difficulty. Then came the Tourmalet, rated beyond category and 2,114 meters high, which was lined for the last five kilometers to the top by fans' parked cars.

With a strong assist from his fellow Z riders, LeMond then began to chase. Not a few other Tours have been won and lost on the Tourmalet, he knew. "No one was doing anything," he said. "Chiappucci was riding the race of his life and no one was chasing him. I had been worrying about Delgado and I decided to forget about him. I didn't think about anything except Chiappucci's lead."

Breukink started to slip back and LeMond repeatedly glanced over his shoulder to confirm that he was leaving the Dutchman behind. Over the Tourmalet, Chiappucci and his group led LeMond by 1:07, down from a high of 2:10 on the ascent. The lead kept dropping as the American towed his group through a steep and sinuous descent with almost no shoulder and a terrifying absence of guard rails or other barriers.

At the bottom, just over 20 kilometers from the finish at altitude, LeMond had sped through the deficit and rejoined Chiappucci. They went up together toward Luz Ardiden, 1,715 meters high and also rated beyond category. With 11 kilometers of the 13.5-kilometer climb left, LeMond tested the Italian by trying to jump off. Chiappucci caught him. LeMond attacked again, only to be caught again. "Each time I rode up to him and looked him in the eyes," the Italian recounted later. "I wanted to say, 'You see, I'm still here, you're not getting rid of me like that.' "

Then came a brave moment for Chiappucci. In a show of force, he went to the front and stayed there for three more kilometers, until Fabio Parra of Kelme attacked and the dozen or so other riders in the group went with him — except for the exhausted Chiappucci. In the sort of savvy teamwork that Z exhibited all day, LeMond's teammate Eric Boyer even swerved the pack away from Chiappucci to make sure he had no nearby wheel to draft.

Seeing this, LeMond rode away with stunning force, followed only by Indurain and Marino Lejarreta. In a few more kilometers they overtook the stage's early leader, Miguel Martinez Torres of ONCE, who had built a lead of 3:50 and been largely forgotten in the battle of contenders raging behind him.

Scenting victory, LeMond grinned briefly as the three left Martinez Torres behind and continued to build their lead over the rest of the 161-man pack. Lejarreta was shed over the final two kilometers, finishing third. As Indurain and LeMond came around the last curve, the Spaniard spurted ahead and crossed the line clapping his hands in happiness.

Indurain started the day in 18th place, mainly because of his nearly 12 minutes lost at Alpe d'Huez in the service of Delgado, and was not a contender for the final victory. The man who was, LeMond, crossed the finish line with neither of the triumphs he had hoped for but, smiling and embracing friends, he made Indurain seem like a sourpuss.

A Man of the Tour

Caught in a traffic bottleneck atop Luz Ardiden, Pedro Delgado had plenty of time to discuss his poor showing in the day's climb. The loss of 1:32 and his eighth place would have pleased most Tour riders, but so much more had been expected of Delgado. With only one more day in the mountains, time was running out for him.

The Spaniard revealed that he had been suffering for a few days with stomach problems. "I wanted to climb with LeMond but I simply couldn't," he said. "Anyway, he was very strong. All that's left for me is a very little chance." More than anything else in the sport, Delgado wanted to win the Tour de France twice. He had long stopped talking about revenge after his tainted victory in 1988, when he slid through a loophole because the masking drug for steroids that was detected in his urine had not yet been banned by the International Cycling Union.

"The fans were very kind to me last year, but there are still some bitter memories," he said before the start of the 1989 Tour in Luxembourg. "I know I have something to prove, and I hope to do so." After winning the Vuelta earlier in the spring, he had spent more than two weeks alone in the mountains, training for the Tour.

But the 1988 Tour had left its mark, surely. How else to explain Delgado's astonishing lateness for the '89 prologue? Pushing his bicycle ahead of him and looking frantic, the Spaniard had arrived at the starting platform 2:40 behind schedule. Quickly he scrambled up the few steps to the ramp and just as quickly mounted the bicycle and pushed off. He finished the day last in the pack as his lateness counted against him. Three weeks later, in Paris, he had barely made up that handicap, finishing third overall.

At the end of the prologue, Delgado explained that he had simply lost track of the time. "I thought I still had a couple of minutes," he said, appearing calm, even joking. Some Spanish journalist disputed his version of what had gone wrong. They said that he had taken a wrong turn when he completed his warm-up near the platform in the center of the city. According to this account, Delgado had ridden nearly a block away from the start, moving through a thick crowd, before a team mechanic caught up with him.

A third, unkinder version said simply that something had shut down in Delgado's thinking, that the pressure of having to defend his yellow jersey had overwhelmed him and left him unable to respond to the ticking clock.

Take your choice.

In the 1990 Tour, the pressure was at first all on LeMond and Laurent Fignon, freeing Delgado. Even now, until today, the pressure had remained on LeMond and Claudio Chiappucci. The early going, the Alps, the transition days through the Massif Central — everybody waited in vain for Delgado to launch the sort of attack that had overwhelmed the pack in 1988. He almost had gotten away on the road to Alpe d'Huez, but not quite. The Villard de Lans time trial was reassuring but again not the crusher it had been two years earlier.

That left only the Pyrenees. "I can afford to give him two minutes there," LeMond judged. "I don't have to worry about him in the last time trial." Delgado insisted, however, that the Pyrenees were not his favorite battleground. "Too close to Spain," he said. "Everybody comes over for the day and the pressure on me is enormous. They all expect me to win and it's hard to ride with that pressure."

Pressure in the Tour was something he should have learned to live with, especially in 1988, when he rode the final week under the threat of losing the yellow jersey because of a time penalty on the drug finding. He was, after all, the consummate man of the Tour: sixth in 1985, well-placed in

'86 when the death of his mother forced him to withdraw, second in '87 to Stephen Roche, a winner in '88, third in '89. He was regarded as hard-working and serious.

An insight was offered by Harrie Jansen, an official of the PDM team that Delgado had ridden for in 1986 and '87. "Delgado was very popular with the team," Jansen said, "even if everybody says, 'We don't really know him.' He doesn't show his emotions. He smiles a lot, but you never know it's really meant.

"Still, he knows exactly what he wants. When he says, 'My season finishes October 7,' you can do what you want, but his season finishes October 7. He's very strong-willed. He's also very open. He demands two minutes after a race for himself — no one can talk to him. He needs two minutes to depressurize. And then he's open to everybody.

"Delgado is the most professional rider I've met, the easiest to work with. You tell him, 'You have to ride this saddle because of the sponsor,' he rides it; 'You have to use these handlebars,' he uses them. He has no pretentions, he's very modest and he lives simply even though he's very wealthy. All in all, an easy guy to handle, a nice person to have on the team."

Spanish journalists had an insight too. When Delgado planned to leave PDM and return to Spain for the 1988 season, he agreed to terms with the Kelme team before the Tour de France but made it a condition that Kelme could not announce his switch until the race finished. That way, he felt, there could be no question of confused loyalties or of team-mates refusing to help a rider who would be leaving.

Near the end of the Tour, with Delgado fighting for the final victory, Kelme decided to get some publicity by letting the news out about his transfer. Charging that his terms and his trust had been violated, Delgado said he would never ride for Kelme and held fast even when threatened with a lawsuit. It became ugly for a while, but this was the sort of pressure Delgado could deal with easily.

Chapter 22

_____ Favorite's Anguish

One and all — riders, team officials, race organizers and journalists — agreed that the Tour had been decided. Refusing to tempt the fates, Greg LeMond was not claiming victory but simply saying, "If I don't fall, if I keep my form, if I continue riding like this ...." While those were a lot of 'ifs,' who could doubt that he was at his best?

Not even Bernard Hinault, who rarely missed a chance to snipe at LeMond in his column in _l'Équipe_. Hinault thought that if an upset was going to develop, it would not be on the next stage in the Pyrenees, from Lourdes to Pau, even if it did pass over the Aubisque Peak, rated beyond category, and the Marie Blanque, rated first category.

Would the Aubisque blow the race open again? Hinault was asked. "I don't think so after what the riders went through at Luz Ardiden," he responded. "I don't think anybody who was crushed yesterday is looking to make any trouble today. Maybe the Aubisque will launch a rider who's trying to win the stage, but no more than that."

He thought even less of the Marie Blanque's potential to dynamite the Tour. "It's so far from the finish," he pointed out. The Marie Blanque lay at almost exactly the halfway

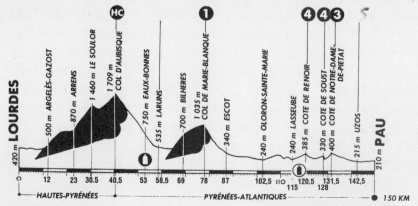

Last day in the mountains: the 22nd stage from Lourdes to Pau.

point in the 150-kilometer stage. After that, the mountains were past.

In a feisty mood after his courageous climb to Luz Ardiden, Claudio Chiappucci had to admit that he didn't think much of his chances either.

"Greg LeMond told journalists that I was finished — well, that was my answer. I wanted to show what kind of rider I am. For the first time in my life, I'm a leader and I wanted to prove that I can be a great leader, a true yellow jersey.

"I know that he's probably going to win the Tour, but he's got a great team and I don't. Five seconds on LeMond, that's not much, probably not enough. I know it. But LeMond better be sure of one thing: He'll have to come looking for me if he wants to find those five seconds."

What brave words Chiappucci spoke, and how true! What a sensible analysis Hinault presented, and how true! What a wonderful sport is bicycle racing, where true words and sensible analyses can be made to fall apart by the tiniest hole in a tire!

For 20 kilometers, LeMond lost control of the race during the 17th stage. Then he and his fellow Z riders rallied to prove the old adage that this is an individual sport practiced by teams. He earned the superb help by subordinating his personal ambitions and working for his teammate Ronan Pensec when the Frenchman was in the yellow jersey.

At Kilometer 77, about 800 meters from the Marie Blanque peak, the rear tire on LeMond's bicycle flatted. "It was my first flat of the year," he said, "and it couldn't have come at a worse time." He was at the front of the pack, chasing a distant breakaway, in a small group of leaders including Chiappucci, Gianni Bugno, Pedro Delgado, and Miguel Indurain, Delgado's locomotive. The climb over the first of the day's two mountains, the 1,709-meter-high Aubisque, had gone without incident.

Two, three, four times Delgado attacked on the 1,035-meter climb up the Marie Blanque and each time LeMond and Chiappucci caught him. And then LeMond had his flat.

He charged afterward that Chiappucci, seeing the flat,

violated etiquette and attacked with Delgado. "I don't forgive him," LeMond said of the Italian rider. "This isn't something I'll forget. One day or another, he'll pay for it." Chiappucci insisted that his attack toward the peak was part of a series of offensives begun by Delgado and denied that he had breached a code of conduct.

Many observers even wondered if, in an age of million-dollar contracts, there really was room in the sport for much etiquette. Attacks after a crash used to be considered a low thing to do and now they are not uncommon. More rare is the attack while riders are stopped at the side of the road to urinate, another violation of the rule in the old days but now just how Joel Pelier won the stage into Futuroscope in the 1988 Tour. An attack in a feed zone provoked acrimony in the first Tour de Trump and yet it has long been a standard tactic in European racing. In short, nobody gets overly upset any more at an attack after a flat.

LeMond's anger had other causes: He was troubled by a deep saddlesore that, along with nervousness, was causing him to lose sleep, especially the nights before the stages in the Pyrenees. It was an extremely hot and muggy day in a week of torrid weather and his feet had swollen and were paining him. Worse, he was alone in the lead group and his team car was far behind him, blocked in traffic on the narrow road.

"It was the first time I had no teammates with me to give me a wheel," LeMond related. "It was the first time the team car was so far behind. It was a lot of firsts."

Another first, or no more than a second, was that Chiappucci was surrounded by four Carrera teammates. "We poured it on," confirmed Acacio da Silva. "It's the Tour and in the Tour you don't give an opponent any presents."

Far behind, LeMond was raging. "I waited, it seemed like hours," he said. Actually it was little over a minute before Roger Legeay, the Z team's *directeur sportif*, pulled alongside his rider. While a mechanic replaced the rear wheel, two Z teammates, Eric Boyer and Jérome Simon, arrived.

"We just couldn't keep up with Greg on the climb," Boyer

said, "and we knew he was isolated. Jérome and I said to each other, 'Let's get going. Greg is alone up there.' Then we heard spectators yelling at us, 'Hurry up, Greg has a flat.' When we reached Greg, he kept saying that he was very worried. That minute it took to get him going seemed like an hour to him. He thought he was losing the Tour. Greg kept saying, 'I've blown it, I've lost the race.' "

LeMond got back on his bicycle but had to stop again after 25 meters because the new wheel was rubbing the frame. This time he was given another bicycle and set off with Boyer and Simon behind him. Chiappucci was over the Marie Blanque and his lead was 1:07.

Far ahead in the breakaway of about 30 low-ranking riders were two other Z teammates, Gilbert Duclos-Lassalle and Atle Kvalsvoll. Using his car telephone, Legeay got in touch with his assistant, Serge Beucherie, who was covering the lead riders, and ordered that they stop and wait for LeMond. For Duclos, this was a heartbreaker, since he was riding for the stage victory in his native region of France. "But, of course, it's part of my job," he said. "I'm nearly 36 years old and I'm going to win my first Tour with Greg. That's worth a chance at a stage victory."

Once over the peak, LeMond led the charge down it. He rode in a frenzy, a man both angry and, as he admitted, scared of losing. "I've never risked my life like that before and I hope I never have to again."

How fast was he going? Jean-François Pescheux, the Tour official who rides a motorcycle and relays time splits between breakaways and the pack, was awed. "I've never seen a descent that fast," he said as he sliced a zigzag with his right hand. "That was the road and LeMond never braked once. He took each curve at top speed. He must have been hitting 80 kilometers an hour. I thought he was crazy." Boyer would never be disloyal enough to question his leader's sanity but he was shaking afterward. "We never touched the brakes," he confirmed, "and we couldn't keep up with Greg."

At the bottom they linked up with Duclos and Kvalsvoll. Taking turns at the front, the five rode a mini-team time trial and soon were in sight of Chiappucci. After a 20-kilometer, 25-minute chase, LeMond was back with the leaders. They stayed together the rest of the way into Pau, where the pack finished 5 minutes 31 seconds behind Dmitri Konichev, who became the first Soviet to win a stage in the Tour.

Later Chiappucci complained that, except for one pull by Indurain on the descent from the Marie Blanque, nobody had been willing to help him and his teammates. "LeMond has a lot of friends in the pack," he charged. LeMond did, and eight of them rode on his team.

He himself insisted that he had not protected Pensec simply out of respect for team etiquette. "No," he said, "it's tactics. It's like a football team: You have players and you have to use the players to your advantage. It's not just short-term.

"I know what the Tour de France is and I had the underlying hope that it would dismantle. One of my better qualities is that I'm very patient and I like to wait things out. But I would never play the same game Hinault did. I know we're a team for three years together and I know that if I want to be able to live with Ronan, we've got to work together. Besides, for me it worked out fine."

Chapter 23
_____ Winding Up the Tour

At the very top, the next two stages leading to the time trial at the Lac de Vassivière were uneventful. Claudio Chiappucci stayed on Greg LeMond's rear wheel from Pau to Bordeaux on the 18th stage and then from Castillon la Bataille to Limoges on the 19th. "It didn't bother me," LeMond said equably. "It's normal. I'd keep him on edge with little attacks, but when there's somebody glued to your wheel, there's no way you're going to drop him by seconds. I figured that it would all come down to the time trial."

LeMond sounded extremely confident. Speaking of the time trial, he said of himself and Chiappucci: "If I lose, I'm going to have a very, very bad day and he's going to have the best day of his life."

While they dueled, a battle for third place developed between Erik Breukink and Pedro Delgado, who led the Dutchman by just seven seconds. That changed on the flat, blazingly hot stage, 202 kilometers into Bordeaux, almost always a field day for the sprinters who have suffered in the mountains for the opportunity of just such a finish.

This time neither of the two men who fought it out could be reckoned exactly a sprinter: Breukink and Gianni Bugno. The Italian broke away with 10 kilometers to go and managed, by a second, to become the first double stage winner of the Tour. What a handsome double it was: Alpe d'Huez, the king of the mountains, and Bordeaux, the queen of the plains. Bugno's victory was the first by an Italian in Bordeaux since 1957, when Pierino Baffi won.

To underline that this was Italy's year in bicycle racing, four of the first five men across the line were Italian: Bugno, Roberto Gusmeroli of Chateau d'Ax third, Giovanni Fidanza of Chateau d'Ax fourth and Adriano Baffi of Ariostea — the son of Pierino Baffi — fifth. For Breukink, the payoff came in the 18 seconds he gained on Delgado to move into third place.

The next stage was another turnaround, with a certified sprinter winning after a long solo breakaway. He was Guido Bontempi, Chiappucci's teammate, who took off with 30 kilometers to go and came home an easy victor. On another day, with a 182.5-kilometer ride through Bordeaux wine country and its greening hills and then into the Dordogne and Perigord, Bontempi would surely have reaped more publicity. Today all eyes were elsewhere, out beyond the suburbs of Limoges and at the Lac de Vassivière.

A Helping Pair of Hands

Whoever said that no man is a hero to his valet never met Otto Jácome. "Besides being a great champion, he's a great person," Jácome says in a typical comment about Greg LeMond. "He does things for other people in a wonderful way."

Then again, Jácome is not exactly LeMond's valet. True, he often looks after his clothes (a Z team racing jersey), makes his lunch (a bag of small sandwiches, some pastry, a banana) and welcomes him home from work with a steadying hand and a drink (a liter-size bottle of mineral water.) Instead, the 53-year-old Jácome is LeMond's masseur, friend and confidant.

"Oh, he's more than that," LeMond said when asked to describe their relationship. "Otto is like my best friend. He's like family. He *is* family."

From the start, the Mexican-American branch of the LeMond family was optimistic about the rider's chances of repeating as champion in the Tour. Speaking in Futuroscope before the race began, Jácome was upbeat: "I think Greg's going to win if he gets some luck. He's in great shape, good health. I know I'm always optimistic about Greg, but I'm not the only one now. He's recuperating very well now."

A few weeks later, Jácome saw no reason to change his assessment. The day before the showdown time trial at the Lac de Vassivière, he said, "When Greg was almost 11 minutes behind, I still knew he was going to win. So right

182

now, when he's five seconds behind, I think he has a 90 percent chance of winning."

Only 90 percent?

"Like Greg says, you can't say 'I'm going to win,' you can't brag about it beforehand," Jácome said. "The only time you can say 'I won the Tour' is when the race ends in Paris. But OK, not 90 percent. Say 99 percent."

Jácome was talking on the side of the road, waiting for the Z team to whiz by and grab the lunch bags he was holding. Afterward he jumped into a team car and sped to the finish line to tend to the riders before going to the team hotel to start on the daily round of massages.

As helpful as they are to relax and tone muscles, aiding in overnight recovery, the massages are hardly Jácome's major asset, LeMond says. "You can get massages by anybody — that's not really difficult to have. You need somebody you can confide in and not worry about it, somebody you can totally trust. I've got my wife and my mom and dad, but Otto is the one who comes on every race with me."

Jácome laughs. "I *am* always with him," he agrees. "I see more of him than his wife Kathy does."

From February through October, Jácome lives a few kilometers from LeMond in Belgium and helps him train by driving a motor pacer. In the off-season, Jácome lives in San Jose, California, where he has been based since 1962, when he first came to the United States from Monterrey, Mexico.

"I met Greg when he was racing as a junior in 1977," Jácome notes. His three sons and a daughter were also racing and Jácome accompanied them as a coach for the San Jose Bicycle Club. "I saw his talent right away and started following him and we became friends. I didn't give him technical advice because we were with different clubs, but I'd see him before a race and give him encouragement."

A former racer himself, Jácome had what he calls "a halfway successful" career. "When I was a junior in 1955, I managed to go to the nationals with the seniors and I finished between 15th and 20th, and at that time Mexico was very strong, so I think I did all right. I raced with racers who were heroes in Mexico and I managed to finish races with them."

He learned the art of massage from his fellow riders. When his children started to race, Jácome resumed the practice and took some courses in California to become an expert. But mainly he was a coach, becoming the Mexican national coach in the early 1980s, when LeMond was beginning his professional career in Europe.

"I lost a little contact with Greg then, but I saw him again at the 1984 Olympics in Los Angeles," where Jácome was leading the Mexican team and LeMond was a television commentator. Invited to work for LeMond, Jácome went with him to the 1986 Coors Classic and then joined him with the PDM team, based in the Netherlands, in 1988. The next year they went to ADR, based in Belgium, and then to Z. While with ADR, Jácome was credited with solving LeMond's problems with undetected anemia.

"It was Otto who thought I looked white, not like myself," LeMond says. After tests, he received iron injections and recovered his strength well enough to go on to win the Tour de France for the second time.

"I consider myself the one who knows him best," Jácome admits. "When I know he's aching, I know he's not going to win."

For all his expertise, Jácome is looking beyond the massage table for the rest of his career. "I'd really like to coach riders, but to come up in the professional ranks, you've got to do whatever they give you. The opportunity is there, you take it." In 1989 he put together a team for Paternina in races in Mexico, then was asked to form a fulltime team for the same Spanish sponsor. "But it was too late in the year," Jácome says, and he declined. Shortly afterward Paternina pulled out of professional bicycle racing.

So, for now, Jácome continues as LeMond's masseur and friend.

"He says he doesn't ever get tired of me," Jácome said.

"I hope he stays with me until I'm done," LeMond said.

Chapter 24

_____ The Showdown

It wasn't close. Greg LeMond sped away from Claudio Chiappucci in the showdown time trial and donned the yellow jersey for the first time since the prologue. Making up his five-second deficit easily, LeMond finished 2 minutes 21 seconds ahead of the Italian.

"Today the Tour is finished," said Erik Breukink, who won the time trial, the 20th stage.

LeMond was still not claiming victory, however, since there remained the final, largely ceremonial ride into Paris the next day.

"I was very strong today," he admitted as he loosened the straps on his shoes and sat to await Chiappucci's finish. LeMond finished fifth in the 45.5-kilometer time trial around the Lac de Vassivière, where he recorded the first stage victory by an American in 1985.

Breukink finished in 1 hour 2 minutes 40 seconds on another scorching day. Second was his PDM teammate Raul Alcala, who trailed by 28 seconds. Then came Marino Lejarreta, 10 seconds further back, with Miguel Indurain two seconds behind him. LeMond was next, 57 seconds behind Breukink, while Chiappucci was 17th, 3:18 behind. He managed to keep second place overall, 13 seconds ahead of Breukink.

"I wasn't forcing it at the end, because I was thinking about the overall standings, not the individual victory," LeMond said. If he had pushed himself over the last few kilometers, he continued, he would have run the risk of exploding — the sudden loss of power and speed that follows overexertion.

Chiappucci showed just such signs near the end as he struggled in slowly. Starting three minutes behind the American, he trailed him by ever-increasing gaps at every checkpoint. At kilometer 10, LeMond was clocked in 14:02 and Chiappucci in 14:13. At kilometer 22, LeMond passed in

29:56 and Chicappucci in 30:27. At kilometer 33, it was LeMond in 43:10 and Chicappucci in 44:27.

When LeMond reached the finish line, Chiappucci was three kilometers behind 'and trailing badly. As the Italian fell six seconds behind LeMond in any possible finish, the news was relayed to the American, who giggled nervously to hear that he was leading the Tour for the first time since it started.

He looked calm and intense at the start, wearing his baby-blue Z team cap backward — en bataille, as the French say, or ready for combat. LeMond disdained most of his usual aerodynamic aids, using a regular road bicycle, not a plunging frame. He rode without disk wheels, but with the same triathlete extension on his handlebars that carried him to victory in the final time trial of the 1989 Tour.

Many other riders used a rear disk wheel and most had the triathlete clip-on bars. Chiappucci rejected both the wheels and the bars. "It all depends on the legs," he said before setting off.

But more than legs were needed. This was a highly technical course, an often-narrow, twisting road with many small climbs and descents. The riders had to make dozens of decisions about when to shift gears while trying to keep as steady a rhythm as possible.

LeMond knew the course well from the 1985 Tour. It followed the banks of the lake only briefly before turning into the hills, where dark copses of pines and scrub oaks cast their shadows onto the road. Neither LeMond nor Chiappucci would have noticed the sidelong vistas as they concentrated on the road. It dipped and turned, rose and fell as it led to the finish and the change in leadership. There were a few boats out sailing on the Lac de Vassivière and here and there some swimmers, but mainly everybody was standing on the side of the road and watching one of the epic stages in the long history of the Tour.

The Road to Paris

Unchallengeable in the lead and glowing in his yellow jersey, Greg LeMond cruised into Paris the next day as the winner of the Tour for the second successive year.

When the 156-man field swept through the last of eight laps on the Champs-Élysées and passed the finish line, LeMond jerked his arms upward in a sign of victory. That gesture is usually left to the stage winner, but the American's jubilance was understandable. Barely three months before, he had been forced to drop out of a minor and short race in Washington because of a combination of undertraining and a viral infection. And now he was once again the winner of the world's greatest bicycle race, three weeks long and covering 3,412 kilometers.

"I was very nervous until I saw the Champs-Élysées," he acknowledged as photographers threatened to overwhelm him. "I almost cried when we reached it."

By finishing 2 minutes 16 seconds ahead of Claudio Chiappucci, LeMond collected a check for about $350,000, which he said he would give to his teammates. "They deserve it," he explained. His feat moved him out of a crowd with two victories in the Tour de France and into the elite company of Philippe Thys, a Belgian who won in 1913, '14 and '20, and Louison Bobet, a Frenchman who won in 1953, '54 and '55. Ahead of them in Tour victories are only Jacques Anquetil, Eddy Merckx and Bernard Hinault, with five each. LeMond says he plans to race three more years.

Unless it is a time trial, of course, part of the final day is traditionally given over to skylarking. In their relief to have made it to the end of the Tour, the riders put aside even the tightest of competitions among themselves, accepting the order that has been determined. So Erik Breukink did not attempt to regain the 13 seconds that separated him from second place, nor Marino Lejarreta the four seconds that separated him from fourth place nor Andy Hampsten the seven seconds that separated him from 10th.

Instead, on the 182.5-kilometer trip from Bretigny sur

Orge, the riders chatted and mugged for the television cameras, with LeMond even raising Chiappucci's hand to show he had forgiven the bitter feelings after the Pau stage. They turned serious only when Paris approached and, with it, the chance for a final piece of glory. Year after year, riders attempt to break away on the Champs-Élysées and steal a victory and, year after year, the finish is a field sprint. So it was one more time after a handful of doomed attacks on the wide avenue lined by 500,000 spectators.

Johan Museeuw, a Belgian who rides for Lotto, won the mass sprint, easily beating Adriano Baffi and Olaf Ludwig. "On every lap I studied the finish," Museeuw said, "and I decided that I had to be in front at the last corner." Coming out of the Place de la Concorde for a final time, Museeuw took the right-hand curve in first position, as planned, and carved a 20-meter lead. He held part of it to the line in what became the only true mass finish of the Tour.

LeMond did not bother to contest the sprint and thus surrendered any chance he had of winning a stage. Not often does a Tour winner fail to pick up a stage victory along the way.

All spring he was criticized for being out of condition and failing to appear in races while wearing the jersey of the world champion. During the Tour, the criticism, mainly by some old-timers, focused on his alleged lack of *panache*, or flair, in not winning a stage.

A typical comment came from Lucien van Impe, a Belgian who won the Tour in 1976. "Greg is a very great racer," he said, "but he hasn't won a stage. He hasn't shown the *panache* of a Merckx or an Hinault."

In rebuttal, LeMond pointed out at a news conference that he finished second in the two biggest mountain stages, Alpe d'Huez and Luz Ardiden. "I think I've dominated this race from start to finish," he said. "If I had worried about individual stage victories, it's possible I would have lost the Tour de France." He finished sixth in the overall points competition, fifth in the mountain competition and eighth in the combativity competition.

"Panache, panache!" LeMond snorts. "It's a race of tactics, not panache."

Sounding more than a mite defensive, LeMond used his news conference to answer his critics.

"There are always people who aren't happy with how you ride and when you ride," he said. "I could ride every race in the world and give half my salary to the poor and I'd still be criticized. There's always that 20 percent who criticize."

Prominent among them had been Merckx. Retired for a dozen years and now a bicycle manufacturer in Belgium, he often takes potshots at today's riders.

"I think Merckx is jealous," LeMond said in what was regarded as a reference to his 1990 salary of nearly $2 million, probably as much as the Belgian earned in a decade. "I'm as good in the Tour de France as Merckx was."

He got no argument from Luis Ocaña, who long competed against Merckx and won the 1973 Tour.

"Is LeMond a great champion?" said Ocaña, repeating a question a few days before the finish. "Good God, I think yes. If he isn't a great rider, what are the others? He's got it all: character, panache and the victories. He's won two world championships and two Tours de France. What more can anybody want?"

Make that three Tours de France now, and counting.

About the Author

Samuel Abt is a deputy editor of the *International Herald Tribune* in Paris and has been closely following the international professional bicycle racing scene since the mid seventies. He has written about the Tour de France for the *Herald Tribune* and the *New York Times* since 1977 and is a regular contributor to *Bicycle Guide* magazine.

Before he moved to France in 1971, he was a copy editor for several newspapers in New England, for the *Baltimore Sun* and the *New York Times*. A graduate of Brown University, he has also been a Professional Journalism Fellow at Stanford University.

His writings include three popular bicycle racing books: *Breakaway*, published in 1985, *In High Gear*, published in 1989, and *LeMond*, published in 1990. In addition, he edited *The Paris Edition*, the autobiography of Waverley Root, to which he contributed the introduction.

List of Available Titles

Title	Author	US Price
The Mountain Bike Book	Rob van der Plas	$9.95
The Bicycle Repair Book	Rob van der Plas	$8.95
The Bicycle Racing Guide	Rob van der Plas	$10.95
The Bicycle Touring Manual	Rob van der Plas	$10.95
Roadside Bicycle Repairs	Rob van der Plas	$4.95
Major Taylor (hardcover)	Andrew Ritchie	$19.95
Bicycling Fuel	Richard Rafoth	$7.95
In High Gear (hardcover)	Samuel Abt	$21.95
In High Gear (paperback)	Samuel Abt	$10.95
Mountain Bike Maintenance	Rob van der Plas	$7.95
The Bicycle Fitness Book	Rob van der Plas	$7.95
The Bicycle Commuting Book	Rob van der Plas	$7.95
The New Bike Book	Jim Langley	$4.95
Tour of the Forest Bike Race	H. E. Thomson	$9.95
Bicycle Technology	Rob van der Plas	$16.95
Tour de France (hardcover)	Samuel Abt	$22.95
Tour de France (paperback)	Samuel Abt	$12.95
LeMond (Random House, h/c)	Samuel Abt	$18.95
All Terrain Biking	Jim Zarka	$7.95
Mountain Bike Magic	Rob van der Plas	$14.95

Buy our books at your local book shop or bike store.
Book shops can obtain these titles for you from our book trade distributor (The Talman Company for the USA), bike shops directly from us. If you have difficulty obtaining our books elsewhere, we will be pleased to supply them by mail, but we must add $2.50 postage and handling (as well as California Sales Tax if mailed to a California address). Prepayment by check (or credit card information) must be included with your order.

Bicycle Books, Inc.
PO Box 2038
Mill Valley CA 94941
Te.l: (415) 381-0172

In Britain: Bicycle Books
63 Ashley Road
Poole, Dorset BH14 0AX
Tel.: (202) 71 53 49

If your book shop does not stock our books, suggest they order them by calling the Talman Company's toll-free number, which they will find listed in *Books in Print*.

The Route of the 1991 Tour de France

(July 6 — 28, 1991)

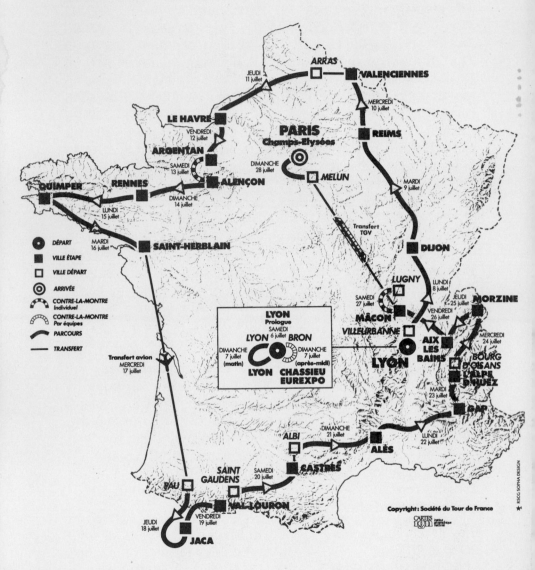